Sonoma Writers Alliance

Anthology
Volume I

Published by SWAPress, Sonoma California
swapressbooks@gmail.com

Printed in the United States of America.

Front cover photograph: Sonoma City Hall by Michael Woolsey, courtesy of Sonoma Valley Vintners & Growers Alliance.
Back cover photograph by William Murray.
Cover design and book formatting by Tom McKean.

ISBN – 0998529219

Reviews . . .

"So often, when asked to peruse the literary offerings of a small town's local Writers Alliance, one is subjected to any number of amateur, introspective journals written for the most part by good meaning and sincere, but rather generic and newly minted middle-agers busily *"finding themselves"* at the suggestion of their favorite therapist. But THIS collection by *The Sonoma Writers Alliance*, much like the town itself, is a real discovery...and treasure."
    — Butch Engle

"It's a delight to read such a variety of offerings from a group of creative, articulate, and dedicated writers who also happen to live in this special community we have here in Sonoma, California. This volume is diverse in the timbre of its voices as well as the genres represented. What a gift these artists have given us!"
    — Monica McKey

"The 2017 anthology of the Sonoma Writer's Alliance entertains and provokes. The prose, beautifully written by the group's thinkers and writers, invites you to "contemplate possibilities where before only impossibilities existed." The poems—ranging from faith, sex and sorrow to truck stops, clowns and unicorns—uncover the hidden. And a one-act play reveals that history doesn't change, only the cast does. A collection worth collecting!"
    — Catherine Sevenau , author of *Behind These Doors* and - *Queen Bee.*

"When a member of the Sonoma Writers Alliance notified me that I was next in line to join the group, I wasn't sure whether or not to do so.... But when I read my first piece, I was comforted and even felt nurtured by how the group held and responded to my words....

Over time I began to realize the marvelous legacy of the group. Two of the founders have been in the group for 21 years and, with others who have joined and left, have formed a container wherein creative expression has been maintained and the fire has continued to burn well into the sunset of life for these writers and thinkers....

Sometimes sitting with the group, I think of how many people could benefit from this amazing beauty. Like entering a sacred garden full of diverse flowers, each one in its own way carries a particular aroma that enchants the senses. How many students could benefit by simply sitting with this group and allowing each flower to take them into the realm of the imagination....

The Sonoma Writers Alliance has created a sanctuary, a place where many souls have found their lives enriched. The creative process fulfills one of the most profound activities of the human endeavor, the capacity to create and recreate life with all its dramas and all its blessings...."

Noris Binet, *A Wonderful Legacy*, 2016

INTRODUCTION

Sonoma Writers Alliance
Anthology
Volume I

*It amounts to this—Literature is not a mere Science, to be studied; but an **Art**, to be practised.*
Sir Arthur Quiller-Couch, 1916

This is the era of the Sonoma writer. At last and again, authorship is lauded as a viable product of Northern Californian art. Somewhere, among the vines, visual arts, music, and digital acumen, Sonoma Valley writers took a several-decades back seat. It's not that northern California didn't *produce* famous writers: there are Jack London, Ursula LeGuin, Octavia Butler, Jack Kerouac, and Amy Tan, among others. Rare, but still visible, were the high quality chapbooks of local writers. But for a while, a lot of Sonoma writers felt as if they sat at the kids' table.

Today, almost completely gone are the frustrations of running out of ink or lined yellow pads. Our days of cursive writing are obsolete, overwhelmed and outdistanced by a bit of silicon, a tiny, almost silent keyboard, and a hunk of plastic with more computing power than it took to get people to the moon and back. What persists is the creative mind.

There aren't a lot of bells and whistles to writing. It is an isolating, quiet, often frustrating effort. It takes forever. It isn't a one-draft-and-you're-done production. Rewriting tests authors like nothing else, and often the family dynamic (little say friends and acquaintances) suffers greatly.

What is worth all this angst and sacrifice? I believe that creating a tangible result from absolutely nothing but one's mind drives many writers. The story can only be told your way, with your ingredients, by you. Writing is the definition of "unique." Its essence cannot be duplicated. It is an accomplishment of individual minds, with a very little cooperation from the rest of the body.

It takes visibility and consistent effort to create a writing reputation for an entire geography, but the Sonoma Writers Alliance has done so since the early 1990s. The group's members created and sustained peer-critiquing authors that include narrative writers, poets, and screenwriters. If you've ever functioned in a workgroup, you know the myriad personal characteristics that rise to the surface. A creative group is 100 times more intense, more artistically and intellectually challenging. Somehow, using a charmed mutual respect and the rare gift of graceful verbal restraint, the Sonoma Writers Alliance makes it work... all the way from concept through and including distribution of printed and digitized work. Having visited the group, and having worked with several members individually, I can attest that there isn't a drop of sameness from one member to another. The points of view, the voices, the structure modeled by each member, are personal and exclusive to each writer.

To their greater credit, the group has birthed a number of other writers' groups. Some have brief bursts of passion for the work; others live long and prosper. Without generous guidance and a sharing of skills from the Sonoma Writers Alliance, none of this would be possible. Members present to groups, speak about their work and process, and mentor other writers. The art of writing thrives in Sonoma via their efforts.

In this remarkable collection, there is a style, a plot, a character, a setting for every reader. This anthology is *a la carte*, with several themes presented by individual voices. Incisive, well-crafted verse and narrative characterize the book. You'll note the care taken by Alliance writers who describe detail with fluidity while still paring irrelevant wording until the reader is left with beautiful, incisive sentences and standout thinking. This is experience and practice honed sharp.

Give a few hours of love for this book the Sonoma Writers Alliance has written for you. You'll find yourself and everyone and everything else you know or didn't know on every page. It was certainly an honor to comment on their accomplishment.

Deb Carlen
Sonoma
January 2017

About the Sonoma Writers Alliance

The *Sonoma Writers Alliance,* formerly known as the Friday Writers Group, was established in 1995 by a group of writers for the purpose of improving their skills and sharing personal writings in poetry, memoir, essay, and fiction.

Some members are award-winning authors, with published works in poetry, fiction, and plays. Others write only for the pleasure of writing. The group meets every week. A different topic is offered to stimulate the creative process, but there is no requirement to write to the topic or prompt.

This *Anthology* is the first collection of submissions from fifteen members of the Alliance. Current and older postings of members' work can be found on their blog, including information about the *Sonoma Writers Alliance* and biographies of the members. Brief bios are also found at the end of the book.

www.sonomawriters.blogspot.com

Author Chapters

● x ●

Russ Bedord

Russ Bedord

Maybe This Spring

Mark fell once on the icy slope leading from the North Wind Bar, which showed he was drunker than usual, though he wouldn't admit it.

"Snow on ice," he mumbled—unusual, because he rarely talked to himself. He just sang—old songs like *Sweet Adeline, O Tannhauser, My Darlin' Clementine,* and *America*—all from his few years of schooling. He occasionally warbled snatches of jukebox tunes absorbed during visits to the bar. He'd catch himself singing one, stop and try to remember where he'd heard it. Unable to finish even one, the old favorites sufficed.

The wind ferreted under his heavy coat and licked his back with an icy tongue. Mark pulled his collar tight, adjusted his scarf to cover his cheeks, and yanked his hat earflaps down to keep out the cold.

Snow blew in swirling clouds, drifting deep. In town it quickly wiped out the footprints of the motorists who had abandoned their cars. In a neighborhood with no street signs, Mark trusted his memory to find a way across the swampy, brush-filled valley to his hillside home.

Most evenings Mark puttered around his three-room shack the way he had for twenty-three years. Often in late afternoon he sipped a whiskey and pondered in a dull way. Problems were never quite resolved. They sat there like stars and other deep mysteries—wells of wonder. When the bottle emptied, he'd stagger to bed. Or he'd fall asleep in a worn, stuffed chair, molded after years of use to his little body. When morning came, he'd nibble something, make his lunch, then hike to town for the ride to work.

Mark had dropped out of school at thirteen. He was small, but wiry and strong, which served him well in numerous schoolyard fights. His slow wit attracted teasing and crippled his replies, so he learned to answer with his fists.

But he hated to fight, so he was attracted to a solitary occupation. Shortly after leaving school, he began pulpwood logging, which seemed the right thing to do. Being alone in the forest by day and home at night was just fine.

It was a happy day when he bought this shack, because it gave him the freedom he wanted. No longer need he be the butt of smart-ass town folks. Their blandishments and arguments quickly passed beyond his understanding anyway. When he felt like washing, he did. When he felt like changing, he did. When he felt like eating, he did. Sausage, bread, turnip, a piece of fish—was enough. Drunken reveries replaced conversation.

But Mark found he couldn't always be alone. The need for companionship led him to spend Saturday nights at the North Wind Bar. The antics of the crowd there provided a kind of entertainment. When the evening's stupor grew with the thickening atmosphere of tobacco smoke and stale beer, he became invisible. He was only interested in the occasional fights, recalling the days when he was at the center of every brawl. When the bar closed, he went home.

Not this night, but on other nights, Mark's rare urges were satisfied by Dirty Bessie. For a drink, she would sit on the next stool, open your fly and play with you until you came. She let you put it away yourself. "Cheaper than a whorehouse" was the nicest thing Mark had heard anyone say about her.

On such a vicious night, the bar was empty. Missing the crowd, Mark drank too much. Only the cold penetrated his drunkenness, and it was hard to walk in the deepening snow.

The hooded view between his hat brim and scarf was a port for the wind-blown snow to hit his skin like icy needles. Beyond, the world was featureless, a blend of dull shades and blinding wind. At first, shallow areas between the drifts gave respite from the heavy going, and the road was partly visible.

He held alive the image of his cozy potbelly stove. He hoped the coals were still smoldering so they could be fired quickly. Thinking of how a house is cold until heated, he shivered. But the shiver was involuntary. Mark was too cold. He tried to walk faster but the drifts had become too deep. Only with great effort could he move.

A song rose to the back of his throat. He opened his mouth to sing, but his jaw didn't work well. The numbness of his face killed the song in birth. The wind would drown it out anyway.

Shivering possessed his body, shaking off the drunkenness, yet his limbs seemed unresponsive. "Goddamn," he said, putting more energy into walking, but it was too cold. The core of him was lonely in its warmth. He hummed to keep it company. The blizzard tore the sound away and replaced it with icy tendrils. He closed his mouth tight, but the cold had already established a firm base in his vitals.

Pushing against the drifts sapped energy. The roadbed had disappeared under the undulating, snowy, gray landscape. Mark found himself in the dense, low brush somewhere off the road. He turned and moved a few steps, but in an unknown direction. Twigs pulled at his clothing. He placed his weight on an apparently solid spot but a buried stem gave way underneath, tumbling him into the snow. A flailing arm swept a twig into his eye. The ensuing tears threatened to freeze.

Too tired now to search for the road, he leaned back into the snow. As he lay there, the ache of the cold grew less and less. He became drowsy, almost comfortable—the situation, after all, did not seem to be of great concern.

He made a sound, a bearlike "hummmm" and "grrrrrr" combined. From his seat in the snow, the blizzard seemed to be passing overhead, albeit only inches. He looked around. Naked sticks of brush poked out of the snow, creating a miniature black forest fading into the greyness. Mark's gloved hand, seeming like someone else's, reached and grasped one. He bowed its black tip into the soft powder. His eyes, and a bicep rubbing against a sleeve, verified the act but there was no feedback from his numb hand.

He laid back and shut his eyes, closing off the sight of the brush clacking soundlessly in the wind. *I can last 'til morning*, he thought, without conviction. *I'll sleep 'til they find me.*

Powerfully drowsy, he imagined his little home, and his old stuffed chair soft as snow. Warm sunlight slants in though the window. The table is set. A hot roast surrounded by steaming potatoes, carrots, and gravy rest in a bowl. Someone is at the door, and he invites them in. It is a crowd, tumbling in like they never have. Mark is comfortable with the invasion—even Dirty Bess is welcome.

It could be like this, Mark thinks as he drifts away, *maybe this spring*.

Epilogue:

They searched for a week, without success, then called it off. Sherriff Hokanson, when asked by a reporter, "When are you going to find him?" said "Maybe this spring."

Sure enough, the spring thaw uncovered Mark's body, a mere twenty feet from the road.

One Should Dream

What is in sleep? What is in dreams?
What is inside, looking for schemes,

Wanting possibilities, wanting things just so—
vowed I would find out, vowed that I would know.

Took my personality, hung it over a chair,
it lay there, silent, passive, like it really didn't care.

Hoped to have a dream I hadn't dreamed before:
in them, I'd be the hero—have the answer, know the score.

But my psyche descended into a dark and threatening place:
searched there for an answer, found mostly empty space.

Somewhere a light is shining in the black,
pointing out prosperity, instead of mostly lack.

Fulfilling my heroic dream, I searched high, searched low,
stumbled on unseen objects, pursued that lonely glow.

Looked everywhere but behind—certainly not within,
'fraid that what I'd find would be like "original sin."

On waking I looked around, personality was still there.
It slipped on so easily, like it really didn't care.

Welcome, it seemed to say. You thought you were gone for good,
but I knew you'd come back, because, you know, you should.

Vibration

While contemplating the light refracting through the ice cubes at the bottom of my glass, a young lady (I discovered later) sat next. "Pour another," I said to the barkeep.

In a dutiful manner he did, looking at me with fake enthusiasm, expecting talk, as most drinkers did. I did not. He looked relieved and sought boredom somewhere else.

"Hi," she said to me. Surprised, I turned to look at her, and discovered then she was comely.

"Hi, yourself," I said, irritated. "I'm used to drinking alone."

"I could see that, *but* I also see that you have a good vibration."

"A good what?"

"Vibration. Vibration is everything—good vibes, bad vibes—all kinds of vibe. Vibe is short for vibrations."

"So my vibe is good, but don't you think you're a little young for me?"

"It wasn't that kind of vibe. It was like a lonely vibe, that you needed someone to talk to."

"Oh," I said, disappointed. I thought that if I were sending out any kind of 'vibe', it would be more likely what I felt than what she thought. She apparently picked up something other than desire for a pick-up.

"Not that I'm against that kind of vibe," she said. "That's what I come here for—but that's not what you need."

Time for sarcasm. "And what do I need?"

"Talk."

"So talk."

She hesitated briefly, then looked around. "Look at the people in here," she said. "They all come here for different reasons, and each sends out different vibrations. It's like when you talk to someone because you know what's on their mind. If you're aware of vibrations, you don't have to talk, just feel and observe."

I picked one. "That man in the gray suit over there."

She stared for a moment, then said. "Poor, poor me vibe."

"You can tell just by looking?"

"From feeling. From feeling, then look to see if anything supports the vibe you feel."

"How so?"

"Look at him hunched over his drink like it was his alone. Probably a recent divorce, or had a falling out with his significant other. And it's all their fault—not his, of course. Otherwise, there goes the reason for feeling sorry for himself. And he nurses the drink like an old grudge. Don't dare mess with his drink, like you couldn't mess with an old grudge. Right or wrong, who knows, because no one ever admits wrong. The hell with him."

A well-built, well-dressed man approached the other side of her and said "Hello." I quickly turned my attention away and focused on other bar attendees, hoping to test her 'vibration hypothesis.' A young couple looked like they were having a good time but they 'vibed' insincerity. Maybe that was it! They thought they should because beer and liquor ads showed happiness if you just imbibed! The way they flaunted their Budweisers suggested I wasn't far wrong.

I hadn't heard more than a few mumbles from the young lady next to me and her male companion, and was surprised to see him stand up, very erect, and walk away without a backward look. To joke, I said: "Not a good vibe?"

"The worst," she said, "the worst. One of those dudes who acts like he's God's gift to women. The vibe he sends is: 'I'm a user, you're a loser, so why don't we hook up.'"

"I thought a hook up was what you were looking for."

"I am, but with a real person, not with a loser who charms, talks nice, looks nice, and pretends to like you but really hates. The purpose is to use, even humiliate women to justify his lousy attitude. Don't worry, he'll hook up with a loser carrying the same vibe. They'll be satisfied for a moment, at least."

"You picked all that up from a vibe?"

"Sad to say, but from experience first. I wasn't the first person to have a rosy view of human nature. Experience taught me to trust the vibe—if it don't feel right, it ain't right."

"What about that young man standing next to the bar over there?"

She stared silently for a few moments. "He doesn't belong here."

"What! He has a firm hold on that beer bottle!"

"Yeah, but the vibe he's sending says: I don't belong, I'm here because I think I'm supposed to be, I look like I'm enjoying myself, but I am not. My guess is that he is from a family where drink had a prominent role to play, but in his life, it does not. Yet, his stance says here I am, look at me, I'm being one of the good guys, am I not? Yet still sipping really slowly, which tells the tale."

I took a long, good hard look at the young man. Her analysis seemed correct, and I turned to deliver a compliment, but she had left only a hand-written note that said: *Nice talking to you.* I spotted her across the bar, sitting next to a lone gentleman. The vibe I got from him was non-threatening.

I got up to say something to her but chose to leave, feeling some satisfaction at having learned something, and a little jealousy at not being chosen by that comely young lady. I need a different vibe.

Clown Value

In that suit of polka dots, however,
And that green floppy hat—I could never
Imagine you having a serious thought.
Wearing such apparel is simply not
Appropriate dress for a weighty word.
Life is a theater of the absurd—
Change depends upon discrimination:
Carefully making evaluation—
Perhaps a concern for worldly affairs
Has you offering your kind of repairs?
Hearing the music in people's laughter,
I see now—that is what you are after.
    But these serious answers I propose—
    Still—that red ball on the end of your nose?

The End of Summer Fun

(Fictionalized Fact)

"Don't move, Marcia! You'll scare it!" Paul crouched to pounce on the frog. It sat, as though waiting to be prodded.

Marcia ran up. "Scare what?"

The frog leaped out of sight into the depths of the water.

"Oh, Geez," Paul said.

"It's just a dumb old slimy thing," Marcia said.

Laying down on a grassy knob, Paul let his body drink in the sun. "I'm tired of tadpoles," he said. "This woulda been my first frog."

"What would you do with it?"

"Keep it in a jar."

"And let it die? It will stink and my Mom will throw it out."

Paul stuck a stalk of grass in his mouth.

"I'll beat you back," Marcia said, and ran, her light dress skimming the top of the fox-tails and timothy grass. Tiny yellow and white flowers whipped to and fro.

She emerged first from the patch of forest. Paul fell in a drainage ditch. By the rickety fence that marked the dead end, they veered to avoid the run-down old house that was last on the street. Marcia tripped on the crab grass infesting the street shoulder, and fell.

"I twisted my ankle," she whimpered.

"Boy, you're dumb," Paul jeered. "Nobody can run on crab grass. It's too lumpy. You should of stayed on the street like me. I'm not scared," he said, pointing at the house.

Marcia sobbed. "If you're not scared, why do you cross over to this side, too?" She limped up to him. "Besides, don't call me dumb. I'm gonna tell."

"I bet you would, baby."

"You're not so old you can call me baby," she said. "Please help. I can't walk."

He guided her to their kitchen stairs.

"Don't go so fast," she said.

He sat her down and plopped beside, peering with exaggerated disgust as she fondled her ankle,

"My mom said to stay away from there, anyhow," Marcia said.

Paul scoffed, but they both regarded the house seriously. Its peeling paint and boarded-up windows on the facing wall made it more drab and darkly mysterious each time they saw it.

A grave expression clouded Marcia's freckled, pert face.

Thinking the whole summer was going to be like this, Paul remembered his excitement when Mom and Dad told him that Uncle Ray would be away all summer commercial fishing, and that Aunt Tina wanted him to spend it it with her and the girls.

"Do you really want to go?" Mom had asked, worried. Sensing her doubt, he ventured a brash, yet insincere reply.

"Spend the whole summer with *girls*?"

"You like Aunt Tina," Dad had added. "You and Marcia always play well together." He smiled and ruffled Paul's hair. "Tina said she wouldn't be lonely with a man around the house."

"She's fun," Paul had said, remembering the games Tina played as his babysitter.

"He's only twelve," Mom had said.

To Paul, it now promised to be an adventure. "She lives by the forest, doesn't she?"

"One house away, and you will be as free as a bird," Dad assured.

"There are farms nearby. Tell him he shouldn't tease the animals," Mom warned.

It was a happy moment when he saw Aunt Tina and the two little girls standing close by her side. She had folded Paul into her bosom. Dad beamed at her compliments. Mom checked out the house and said she was satisfied that he would be comfortable.

"You don't have a phone," she complained to Tina.

While Tina wrote down the neighbor's phone number, Mom and Dad patted and groomed Paul as seriously as confirmation, then admonished possible behavior. "Help Tina as much as you can," they had said. Dad's jaunty demeanor and Mom's concerned expression stuck in Paul's mind when they drove away.

When Tina showed him his bedroom, he rushed to the window, eager to see the woody playground. Leaning dangerously out, he caught a glimpse of forest, and beyond, green pastures dotted with tiny cows. Most of the view was blocked by the house at the end of the street. He ran to the other bedrooms, the kitchen, and to the dining room, but to no avail—the view was blocked. Even from out in the yard, a gnarled apple tree prevented a reasonable view.

Paul and Marcia spent almost every day in the forest. Every day they ran quickly past that house, avoiding its tomb-like air. Once past, they played in the magic garden of forest. Frolicking in the dusty heat of summer days, they conducted exciting imaginary expeditions in which they assumed the roles of a catalog of heroes. A failed voyage on a water-logged raft built by earlier adventurers was soon forgotten in the diversions of the teeming life in and around the pond. Fresh deer tracks teased their imaginations every morning with the possibility of glimpsing one of those elusive creatures. Blackbirds perched on slender stalks of grass without bending them. Paul tried to deplete the pond of tadpoles, with little success, for they offered their wiggly black bodies in new multitudes. Sometimes the children just laid in the sun-spotted shadows beneath the greenery, inspecting insect life and listening to their myriad sounds. They resolved many issues but were puzzled by even more.

One day, Paul saw a pinched face peeking from behind the sagging curtains of the old house in the window facing the forest.

"Who was that?" he asked Tina.

"Hilda. The woman. The old man wouldn't be home now."

"What old man?"

"Borg—but don't concern yourself about him. You're usually in bed long before he comes home."

Tina closed the subject by tending to some duty or other. "Paul, get some firewood!"

Paul jumped to the chore. Marcia limped after him. "Stay away," he said, "you'll get hurt."

She leaned against the chopping block.

"Get outta here," he said, possessively yanking the ax out from the chopping block.

She didn't move.

"Aunt Tina," Paul shouted, "Marcia won't get away!"

Tina shouted back: "Marcia, you could lose a finger!"

Marcia resentfully slammed the kitchen door.

"Gonna do girl's work," he taunted, then jerked with surprise as the old woman from next door skittered down their kitchen stairs. In a moment, her frail body passed by the apple tree and out of sight. Paul stared at her disappearance as though hypnotized. He shook himself and returned to work. A sturdy boy, he attacked the woodpile, working up a prideful heat. With pieces of wood cradled high in his arms, he felt his way across the yard and up the kitchen stairs. Tina opened the door and the wood-box lid. He tumbled the burden into the box with a crash.

"My, you carry almost as much as your Uncle Ray," Tina said and gave him a chocolate kiss. "Better get cleaned up for dinner."

After grace, Paul asked about the woman.

"Mom gave her something," Marcia said.

"What?" Paul asked. The woman's furtiveness was mysterious.

"A loaf of my bread," Tina said.

"Was she begging?" asked Marcia.

"What makes you think that? She just wanted to borrow flour."

"Don't she have none?" four-year-old Anne piped up.

"Not very much of anything, it seems. She borrows a little bit of this, then a little bit of that. One day she asked for two sugar lumps. 'What for?' I ask. 'Coffee,' she says. 'Have coffee with me,' I say. She says 'No.' She then returns exactly what she borrows, every time. I say 'keep it,' she says 'No'."

"How come she took the bread?" Paul asked.

"That's the first time." Tina spooned out potatoes. "Old Borg is so cheap, he gives her enough money to buy a little at a time. She hides falling short by getting it from me, and I guess she's not supposed to. Let's eat now."

Paul heard a noise at the window and looked up to see Borg's grim visage. "Look," he said.

Tina opened the kitchen door. The man shoved the remainder of the loaf at her and said, "We don't need your bread," then turned abruptly and marched away.

"He looks mean," Marcia said.

"Stay away from him," Tina warned.

"How come we never saw him before?" Paul asked.

"If you stayed up later, you'd hear him coming home—drunk most of the time. That poor woman, I feel sorry for her: constantly living in fear." Her expression became thoughtful, then resolute. "I know she needs a friend. He doesn't frighten me," she said.

"He frightens me," Marcia said in a small voice.

"Me, too!" Anne chimes.

"Scaredy cat babies," Paul said.

Offended tears rose in Marcia's eyes.

Shush, now, children," Tina said. "Finish your dinner. That's no way to talk, Paul."

They flinched at the distant slam of the Borgs' door.

Shortly, indistinct sounds like curses issued from that house. As darkness grew, the noise filled the air. Paul heard the girl's bare feet padding into Tina's room and her soft reassuring tones. The monstrous passion of Borg's railing continued. Thumping sounds penetrated the blank wall.

The summer wore on. Soon hundreds of little green fruits decorated the apple tree. Ripening into crimson-yellow globes, they looked like gaudy Christmas bulbs on the cheapest and meanest-looking tree around.

Paul stopped one day to sample one. Their colorful roundness against the dark branches made them too luscious to resist. He picked one. The recoil of the branch shook some loose. One rolled onto the street, looking lush on its black surface. He tasted the apple. Its firm flesh still had a slight sour green taste. The ripe softness creeping into its texture promised the sugary flavor of a truly delicious fruit. He picked more to stuff his pockets, shaking dozens loose They ricocheted down through the branches, sounding like a wooden pinball machine. He smiled happily at Marcia.

She was on the kitchen stairs, staring apprehensively and waving a warning. Paul turned to go, but was blocked by an expanse of shabby clothing. He lifted his eyes to see the dour face of Borg, who mumbled something he didn't understand. The man's face transfixed Paul. Its creases, like folded concrete, framed brutal features. The jaw hung open, and the mouth was pulled back in a lipless grimace through which Paul saw a row of ragged brown teeth. Borg's nose infected the face with a rigidity that expressed heartless cruelty.

Borg stood, his knobby hands reaching slightly, then stopped, staying quiet and steady. His eyelids blinked slowly over pale eyes.

The apple went dry in Paul's mouth. He tried to spit it out, but suddenly realized that if he did, the pulp would land on the man's clothing. Paul was consumed by the thought that he would not want that to happen, because the clothing would actually dirty the pulp. He swallowed. A chunk of apple hurt his throat. Moving mechanically, he emptied his pockets, then sidled around Borg, his limbs moving awkwardly. Borg remained motionless, bent toward the spot Paul had left. He turned his head, oddly limber, to Paul, which triggered the boy into flight. He careened up the stairs and into the kitchen. He sat on the wood-box, panting, not really knowing what he felt.

Paul and Marcia rarely saw Borg, but they returned cautiously from play, sure he would appear. They avoided the apple tree. Undisturbed, the apples ripened, their rotten pulp littered the ground, enjoyed only by flies and worms. When Borg appeared, the children disappeared quickly. Paul, especially, was super aware.

He often couldn't fall sleep until he heard Borg, who usually came home in the half light of dusk, or in the dark. Paul tossed and turned until then, feeling uneasy and unsafe. Fighting sleep, he'd prop his chin on the windowsill and wait for Borg's passage. The last streetlight, four houses away, was obscured by heavy elms, making it difficult to see. Many nights, Borg passed soundlessly in the black. The bang of his distant door-slam jolted Paul. After the cold flutters in his chest subsided, he'd drop off to sleep. Some nights, Borg, probably drunk, stumbled off the pavement. The scraping of gravel and muttering were the only clues he was there.

He muttered in a strange language, the words floating in the damp night air. Their malcontent tone filled the bleakest chinks in the shadows. Borg's tirades usually punctuated those nights, their violence threatening to burst the blank wall. The noise stretched Paul's wakefulness to exhaustion. He'd fall asleep, only to be jarred awake by Borg's manic, noisy persistence.

The lack of sleep in the growing heat of summer made Paul irritable. He began to harass the girls and bicker. Tina asked if he was all right. His response was grumpy and listless. Jutting his chin defiantly, his jaw, which had promised to be a prominent feature, was softened by the turned-down corners of his mouth.

"You're not enjoying yourself," Tina said.

"It's a lot of fun out by the pond."

"As much as I enjoy having you here, I want you to be happy. Do you want to go home?"

This suggestion was appealing, and he almost said yes, but he felt he had an obligation to fill, and would be letting Tina down by leaving.

"No," he said, fixing his eyes on her with sad conviction.

One hot day in late summer, Marcia and Paul returned early from playing, bushed by the oppressive afternoon heat, and found Tina and Anne napping. Marcia joined them. Paul split a small load of firewood, then drove the ax lackadaisically into the chopping block. As he filled the wood-box, someone knocked hesitantly on the door. He opened it to be confronted by the miserable appearance of the old woman.

"Tina," she said, turning her head abjectly to the side. A tatty shawl partially veiled her face. She tried to pinion the ends of it, but the movement became an ineffectual pawing at her worn dress. Her feet, planted in rough oxfords, had a mystic quality of movement, like the quiet alertness of a bedraggled and beaten wild thing ready to take flight at the slightest danger. Her face showed the sickly yellow trace of bruises. Paul was flooded with mixed feelings of fear, pity, and curiosity. She lifted her dull gaze, startling him into action. He got his aunt.

"A cup of sugar, please," she said, and produced a dented metal measuring cup from somewhere in her dress. Tina filled it to heaping.

"There you are, Hilda. Anything else?"

"Thank you. I'll return this."

"I know you will. Are you all right?"

"Yes," the old lady mumbled, and left.

"He beat her bad," Tina said.

"Is he crazy, Aunt Tina?"

"She's a prisoner. Poor woman."

"Why doesn't she call the police?"

"She's afraid to."

"I bet they'd put him in jail."

"I wish they'd put him away permanently," Tina said.

When Paul mentioned the visit at dinner, Tina shushed him, indicating that she didn't want to talk about it in front of the girls.

Restlessness pervaded the house that evening. When darkness fell, a cool wind started blowing, canceling the heat of the afternoon. Tempers were short and the girls fought going to bed. Tina finally prevailed, but their squabbling continued upstairs.

While Tina washed the dishes, Paul stood by the unlit bay window staring pensively at the yard, kitchen stairs, and kitchen door. Clouds scudded across the moon, plunging the yard into darkness. The breeze whipped the apple tree to and fro, its branches scratching the wall of the tired old house. Paul thought he heard its distant door slam and felt a twinge of sympathy for the old woman.

A movement near the apple tree grew into a shape that charged across the yard and up the kitchen stairs. It was Borg. In the yellow light leaking from the kitchen, Paul saw the tortured workings of his face. He seemed to be trying to talk, but no sound choked out of his pulsating throat. He moved his arms with violent, yet inhibited gestures. The flesh around his eyes was tense, but stiff. With visible effort, Borg quelled his agitation. Paul imagined he saw Borg's eyes glowing red. From a set stance, Borg reached out and woodenly knocked on the kitchen door.

Suddenly afraid, Paul shouted, "Don't answer!"

"What's wrong," Tina said.

"It's him! It's him!"

Tina peeked out. "Oh! Now what does *he* want?"

She opened the door, and it was like opening the gates of hell. Galvanized by the light streaming from the kitchen, Borg's agitation returned, accompanied by mad shouting in the same alien tongue of his mutterings. Tina waited, but the hysteria increased.

"I can't understand you," she shouted.

His chattering mounted.

"Speak English!" she screamed.

He clattered on.

"What's your problem?" Tina outshouted him, her face reddening.

He raised his arm, threatening to strike.

"To hell with you!" she said, and slammed the door.

Borg immediately became silent and motionless. Then he reared his head back, raised his arms with fists clenched, and bellowed an animal roar. He turned, and descended the stairs in a headlong motion. At the bottom, he stopped, rigid and silent again. With feet planted, he turned with awkward, stiff, fast movements to glare at the door repeatedly. He then wandered around the yard, mumbling what sounded like curses. When he passed into the glow from the kitchen, Paul saw his eyes gyrating, the whites flashing, and his mouth working insanely—now with pursed lips, now gaping. Foul sounding words boiled out with manic energy.

Tina turned out the lights, saying, "If he thinks we've gone to bed, he'll go away."

Borg disappeared in the direction of the woodpile. The muttering ceased.

"Mommy, what's that noise?" The girls, wide-eyed, had come downstairs.

"Go back to bed," Tina said.

"No. We're afraid."

"Go on. We're all going to bed, anyway." Her anxiety was apparent.

The girls did not move.

Paul strained to see. Borg reappeared and stomped back up the kitchen stairs. Something in his hand flashed as he brought it down with a crash on the door and shouted in that strange language that sounded like threats.

"He's got the ax," Paul screamed.

"Oh, my god, stop him!" Tina hid the girls behind a barricade of chairs.

Paul had one thought: stop Borg. He desperately looked around for a weapon. The wood-box. He grabbed a piece of wood and crouched by the door. "If I can hit him before he sees me...," he said, unaware he had spoken aloud.

He crouched, tense, still, waiting, ready to strike, and flinched at each terrible jolt on the door. The rending sound of the ax and rushing in his ears overwhelmed the senses. He expected the door to burst. A glance at Tina and the girls emphasized his awful responsibility. When Borg burst in, they were going to die.

Paul remained crouched, weapon ready. He had no choice. He could not run. Each blow on the door jarred him to another level of apprehension, to a level beyond tolerance. Tension peaked, then petered out. Its absence made a dead place deep inside. The deadness sat like a heavy stone—that became a rock of cold determination. No other feeling existed. The coldness suffused his body, bringing with it a desolate calm. He felt comfortable, almost fluid and capable. Surroundings and the circumstance appeared to be at a distance, clearly etched and observable, like a movie.

If something funny happened, he could laugh out loud. He guessed that Tina might think him crazy if he did. He saw her body spread out in front of the girls like a chicken over chicks. They peeked between the openings of the chairs, their eyes shadows in the pale ovals of their faces.

He noticed that the axing had stopped. With pulse pounding loudly in the silence, he listened. Borg seemed gone. Paul cautiously placed an ear against the door. Tina started to say something, but he quieted her with a violent gesture. He recoiled at hearing Borg's gasping breath, fully expecting the ax to blast through the door and down on him. After a few moments, he listened again. The breathing was less labored now, less out of control. Borg cursed, then stomped down the stairs.

After a while, Tina crept to the window and looked out. "He's gone," she said, her breathy announcement punctuated by the slam of Borg's distant door.

Paul was wrung out. He responded mechanically when Tina herded the family out the door to the neighbor's. He peered fearfully around the yard and was startled to see the ax returned to the chopping block. He stared harder, not sure of the sight. When the clouds released the moonlight again, yes, there it was.

Tina called the police. They slept at the neighbor's. Next morning, only dimly aware of a whirling discussion, Paul toyed with his food. When encouraged to eat, he wandered into the living room instead and sank deep into a soft chair.

Tina leaned over him. "Mom and Dad are coming. Everything is going to be all right," she said softly.

Paul looked into her eyes and appreciated the concern he saw there. It was pointless to discuss what had happened, and horrible to contemplate what could have happened.

"The police have him," she said.

Keep him away, Paul thought, and shivered. He took a sweet roll she offered, but just held it and sank deeper into the chair. Through a window, he saw the apple tree, the house at the end of the street, and a bit of the forest. A morning fog had condensed from the pond and spread, obscuring everything. Shapes were gray and blurred, as though seen through frosted glass.

Noris Binet

The Magnificent – The Last Great Whale

One shining morning I was standing on a deck looking at the waters of the Pacific. I don't recall how I got there but because the ocean holds the purity of all forms for me and a sense of wonder, its vastness always takes me in as if I am a newborn, full of amazement. There is no particular time for me to be at the ocean; any time is a great time. When I cannot be there for a long while, it's as if I am being deprived of life's sustaining energy.

At the ocean I feel that I am before the beginning of all of life's creation. On this auspicious Sunday I was alone but aware of people moving about in a holiday spirit on the wharf, browsing the restaurants and shops nearby. Suddenly, right in front of me, a couple of medium-sized whales, appeared jumping and playing. I was delighted just to watch them as they moved freely, frolicking in the waters with so much ease. I was only fifteen to twenty feet from the young mammals and the deck was only a few feet higher than the water. When they slipped back below its surface, I stood mesmerized by their beauty, their sleek skin and the magnificence of their sheer size. How lucky, I thought, to be able to witness them that closely, almost in reach of my hand!

I felt so privileged at that moment, realizing that I was part of...and before I could finish the thought, I was impacted by the force of a huge, archaic marine creature, which emerged from the ocean with such might that the water spilled out from her jump, wetting my face and drenching my clothes. I was awestruck and thrilled to be in the presence of such an amazing being, before whom I could neither move nor do anything and thus became absolutely still at such greatness and wild presence. The wetness covering my face felt glorious, as if it was a baptism of some kind, and now I realize that it was just that! This magnificent creature from the mysterious depth had baptized me.

Her mammoth proportions overwhelmed my senses to such a degree that I knew I could never be the same after this startling encounter. It is impossible to meet "the magnificent" without being transformed! What is this? Who is this? My questions fell away as my eyes were transfixed upon her, being totally hypnotized by this grandiose energy that felt so primal and ancient as the original mother of all life. I was fully present and entered into a timeless-time, without beginning or end, realizing that that moment is still here with me now.

I wanted to capture her in form and be able to see her image over and over. This fascination overtook me so that I couldn't help but take a pencil and begin to sketch her from memory. Despite my immediate self-doubt about replicating her form, the magnificent creature emerged from the paper without struggle exactly as she appeared to me, spontaneous and free. Drawing her allowed me to be with her and to see the details that were imprinted in the depth of my psyche, without me even knowing it. Amazing revelations have begun to happen as her primordial energy continues to take form, communicating slowly why she came to see me.

I am unable to unveil the details of her communication because it is a process that is unfolding intra-psychically and thus can't be named or conceptualized. It can only be felt. And the feeling seems to be like a resurrection, as if deeper, dormant forces have begun to resurface and lead me through a world of symbols, the meaning of which can only be revealed when experienced, not before. And, as if I am moving in the unknown, only following inner impulses, before the defining thoughts of what is happening have emerged in the mind.

As I began to research whether anyone had seen this particular being before, or whether there are tales about her, I found that no one had seen her exactly as she appeared to me. I discovered that whales are often associated with the wisdom and awareness of the inner spiritual realm, wherein the conscious and the unconscious are blended into an undivided wholeness.

Throughout my life I have felt compelled to dwell in the depth of the psyche. I have come to realize that as I navigate in the emotional depth of the unconscious world, I can swim with "the magnificent" without being totally overwhelmed by her power. Instead, I am guided by her beauty and serenity. When I am able to allow her energy to express itself in me, I can move without resistance in the fluidity of this life. I can come out to breathe and the experience of the breath can be a moment of illumination.

The great whale came to me knowing what is necessary for my maturation to unfold and to guide my entry across the threshold of my own transmigration. Her energy brought about my realignment with the full expression of creativity and spiritual awakening as the ultimate purpose of this life. She was the last archaic, gigantic whale wandering, looking for me in the great vastness of the ocean, and now we are together. Now, she has come home. She lives deeply within me and within you, ready to be activated, embracing us as *The Magnificent*, the great Mother of all.

Divine Self

Divine Self
myself, yourself
we are one,
not two, or three or four
but just One
Illuminating the heart!

Kissing You Back

Have you ever kissed a rose
and let its breath
infuse
your nostrils
with the secret aroma
of life?

Have your lips gently touched
the petals
of a bright red rose
allowing both textures
to recognize each other?

Let me know...
because then we can
share the secret
delights of the divine
presence
that is kissing you back
all day long.

The Wonder of This Earth

As a young child the earth was a land of unimaginable surprises, full of mystery and secrets. Where the chickens laid their eggs was one of those secrets. To find their hiding places was a path of watching and adventure. After several days following them around, I found some clues, but it was still difficult to reach the nests. Passing through intricate branches with many thorns at the edge of a cliff, where a slip would send me rolling down to the river with bruises and torn flesh, was quite a challenge. My quest was usually rewarded because most of the time I was lucky enough to find several eggs.

Everything had a sense of adventure, like going underneath the woodhouse floor, not to encounter smelly, dead creatures, which inevitably rested there, but to find valuable coins since that old shack was the first store in which my parents sold food items and merchandise. While uncovering money down there I would find little baby-blue tarantulas that had been born just a few days before.

Walking outside the gate was also an enchanting phenomenon for me. Honeybees with their humming sound—a melody that soothed my senses, announcing that they were there moving, working and alive. I remember with so much clarity the honeycombs, oozing out the golden, thick liquid, the ambrosia of my childhood.

My whole world was filled by the wonder of an earth that was alive and thriving everywhere I looked. The trees held a marvelous delight that sweetened my senses with just one bite into the sparkling, shining, reddish-green skin of a ripe, juicy mango. It seemed that the whole world was glowing around me like fireworks in the sky, luminous and exhilarating. Uncertain, tender sprouts appeared from nowhere, yet steadily reaching toward the sun. Oh, what a life was mine; pregnant with so much potential everywhere I looked and played.

In every hidden corner under bushes galore, I could become as tiny as a spider and squeeze myself into the amazing world of roots, dead leaves and amazing insects of many varieties and sizes. I was mesmerized by how the land enraptured me, enveloping my mind just as caterpillars were wrapped up inside a leaf to begin their important journey of transformation. Like these mysterious creatures, I too had to hide my innermost precious self to protect me from the emotional and turbulent family environment that was also part of my childhood. So I surrounded and encircled my inner person with layers and layers of reactive mechanisms: toughness, smartness, uninhibited charming attitudes all relied upon to survive, so that one day I could safely go inward and begin the journey of self-discovery, much like so many creatures unburying the precious seeds that they had hidden underground a long time ago.

Land so full of wonder was the foundation of my life, but that too got buried as I moved into an urban setting that prized predictability more than spontaneity, linear order more than the circular, spiral unfolding of nature. Slowly I began to forget what life, connected-to-the-earth and full-of-creatures was like and which was now becoming unseen through my growing-up eyes.

As an Islander I realized that whatever direction I traveled on land would soon bring me to the ocean, and a rapid end to further movement. I can't explain the mind of an Islander beside the idealized notion of having a free and easy-going nature. However, I can sure speak to the shift I experienced when I migrated away from my Caribbean island to a vast, seemingly endless land. My experience of the earth became enhanced and enriched. There was a sense of interconnectedness wherein I felt I could walk and walk until reaching *la Tierra del Fuego* (the Land of Fire), in the southern hemisphere or travel northward to the Arctic ice fields. It was a new sense of freedom to move and expand my horizons almost indefinitely without ending too soon at water's edge.

Then as I began to travel further across more land and oceans halfway around the earth to Indonesia, exactly opposite from the island of my birth, there was a new experience of the earth as a true planetary orb. Though it was the same deep, humid heat found on my own island, here the senses were awakened in entirely new ways, both through the unfamiliar terrain and the exotic culture, a culture which everywhere displayed a vital relationship between people and the land through rituals, ceremonies and shrines honoring the mysterious forces of nature. There, a new doorway into a deeper understanding of the hidden, spiritual nature of the earth began to open for me.

Then during my next trip abroad, this one to India, I came to understand how we are intricately connected to the movement beneath our feet and over our heads. Almost all of the Western women who traveled to India experienced two menstrual periods in the space of a month. Soon we realized that our journey to the other side of the globe impacted our bodies such that we naturally responded to the movement of earth and its lunar satellite and our countermovement through the air. That same trip abroad brought me to the source of the Ganges River in the glacial terrain of the Himalayas at a height that I still find hard to believe I ascended. We arrived in the late afternoon to a place of shelter, but couldn't continue the last three kilometers to the glacier because the air was too thin to support the oxygen needed by our bodies.

I woke up the next morning to see sharp, rocky peaks, dressed by piercingly white snow, reaching up into the sky. I stood speechless and was awestruck by the surrounding beauty. There was such a crude, unadorned, direct connection to this mountain that my wide-open heart soared, such that the experience still resonates within me today. I had ascended to the holiest place on earth for many Hindus, where thousands of pilgrims ascend every year to be in communion with what they deem to be the source of life.

A sense of sacredness permeated the atmosphere created not by human hand but by the earth itself in pure and virgin manifestation. When I reached an unexpected crystalline pool of water that sparkled like a turquoise jewel in contrast to the surrounding terrain and saw the snow peaks and the river off in the distance, I felt the divine essence of life where beauty is the only language needed to convey such truth and wonder. The wonder of my childhood came through, not by the smallness of life beneath bushes and inside of beehives but by this world's largest and most defiant mountain range.

Vultures

Do not be horrified
by the vultures
eating a corpse!

They are cleaning
the earth!

Buitres

*No te asustes
por los buitres
Comiéndose un cadáver*

*Ellos están limpiando
la tierra!*

Come Dance with Me

Come, come dance with me
and play with the sky.

Do not let this life pass
in sorrow, regrets and unfulfillment;
do it now
while you are breathing
and the sky is blue and the earth
is brown.

Take this chance
right this minute
and give yourself permission
to be happy
without reason or with nothing to gain.

Just for the sake of it
experiment with being joyful
even when nothing has changed
and you may be in pain
or have no security at all!

Be like me for a moment
letting the sky fall in pieces
and the earth be uncertain of my steps
not knowing when or where I will end up
but taking the chance
for once
to be fully nothing at all!

Dance with Your Shadow

Dance, dance, dance
with the shadow of yourself
run naked under the rain
and let your skin touch the wind

Bathe in the waters of your dreams
and wake up
with nothing to hold on to
be the child that does not speak
but smiles at the sun

A revolution is taking place
do not wait till it is over to catch on.
It is simple
if you are willing to dance now.

Dance , dance with your shadow
run naked under the rain
and let your hair
flow with the wind
wild, impractical, unpredictable, free!

My Grandmother's Healing Touch

How can anyone really explain the healing touch from the hands of a beloved grandmother—a touch that energized every fiber of your body, transforming you in ways that will continue to support your entire life? Such was the touch I received from my grandmother when I was just a young girl. When in the middle of the night a child suffers from a high fever in the countryside of an island nation, where no doctor or nurse is available, there is only one resource that can work when urgently needed, and in time.

I remember that evening my mother had been trying all kinds of remedies to stem my high temperature, but nothing worked. I have a memory of lying down on my bed and hearing soft murmurs around me, people passing close to my bed, stopping, putting their hand on my body and saying the words *"no, la fiebre no ha bajado"* (no, the fever has not come down), then having my mother slide the thermometer into my mouth. My body was on fire and the discomfort made me groan frequently with pain.

With my mother's remedies unable to break the fever, I suppose it was then that my grandmother was summoned from her house. She lived only a five-minute walk away at her age, but 30 seconds for me when I was running around like a wild cat. At first I didn't know that it was my grandmother, Mama Carmela, touching me. What I do recall was the softest touch that you can imagine as she took my naked body and caressed it from top to button and bathed it with a soothing and comforting touch, transporting me to a place of feeling profoundly cared for. I don't recall hearing her voice but I sensed her speaking to me deeply in a way I had not experienced before.

She applied an *unguento* (ointment) that cooled my body, and calmed the fire within, finally allowing me to breathe more freely while relaxing my whole system. I felt completely embraced in her love. It was a warm embrace where my whole body was enveloped with a kind of vibration that I can't really express more clearly than that.

Mama Carmela was a woman of strong character; she was straightforward and ruled her household with great order and efficiency. Even as strict as she appeared, she never yelled at us or even raised her voice that I can recall. I always knew what to expect with her clear and direct ways, which, as I look back upon now, I realize I deeply appreciated because I knew exactly how to behave in her presence, not like in my own home where I was often punished for my behavior, with the rules seemingly vague and capricious.

She took a daily nap sitting in her rocking chair in the dining room in front of a window facing the pathway to her mother's house, my great-grandmother, Mama Toñi. Our houses were in separate compounds next to each other, so for me to be able to go to Mama Toñi's house, I had to pass through my grandmother's compound. Very often, exactly at the time Mama Carmela was having her afternoon siesta, my siblings and I would try and sneak across her compound to play with some of our cousins. We would squat down so that she couldn't see us through the window, but usually before we could pass by, her voice would come out from the house with the typical question: *Quien va*? (Who's there?). No one would answer! Again the question, *Quien va*? At this point we learned to answer and she would say "come here" and would give us each a piece of candy and send us home with her rebuke that siesta is not the time to be visiting anyone's home or for children to be running around disturbing the quiet. And that was that! Today we laugh at her ways and rejoice that we had such a precious grandmother.

Mama Carmela possessed a natural elegance in how she walked, moved, dressed and behaved. Her weekly trip into town to have her hair and nails done was a sacred duty. Her place in the world was well-defined. As a country woman she was rooted in the rhythm of nature and she was bound by her family obligations. Her life seemed to be as natural as life itself, from the leaves she cut from the orange tree for her evening tea, to her rising from sleep with the morning sun and enjoying her homegrown, freshly ground coffee. An interwoven relationship existed in her home between human, animal and plant life, where cats ran around looking for food and chickens crossed into her living room looking to expand their day by walking on the cool, colorful, Italian-mosaic floor of her house. The surrounding porch of her home was adorned with beautiful, ornamental plants and multi-colored flowers. All together the setting displayed a rich, harmonious environment, where everything and everyone seemed to thrive.

I am not sure how long Mama Carmela's massage of my body lasted. Was it a few minutes, an hour, or perhaps the whole night? Everything felt blurred and fuzzy and I began to feel lighter, as if I had been emptied out of whatever had happened to me. Through my grandmother's healing touch, the fever dissolved gradually throughout the night as the vapor emanating from the ointment penetrated my pores and brought cooling relief.

As the new day broke onto the horizon, my well-being returned and I woke up fully alive and restored. After that night Mama Carmela was no longer just my grandmother, but now I looked upon her with a sense of awe and wonder with her magical capacity to touch lives in restorative and transforming ways. She became greater than my own mother, possessing mysterious qualities that elevated her to the rank of the archetypal Great Mother.

Over the past forty years, as I have traveled back and forth to my island home, I have witnessed how the aging process produced deeper and deeper wisdom and grace in my grandmother. She relaxed her strict character of earlier years, laughed at the nonsense of the pretensions around her and passed on to me simple teachings that were direct and clear. A profound communion developed between us as we shared from our mutual stores of gained wisdom, hers by a deep connection with her place, from which she never moved, and mine from experiences of new cultures, exotic environments and world travels.

Once, after a shamanic ceremony, which I led for Mama Carmela and her sister, my great Aunty Titatina, I was humbly astonished that they referred to me as a sister. During the ritual a triangle of energy was created between us that profoundly deepened our spiritual bond and connected us at a level that would never be broken. For the last ten years before my grandmother died, she appeared to me repeatedly in dreams, preparing me for her death, energetically transmitting to me more and more of her wisdom, and she became my Zen master. Finally at the age of 101, and at the end seeming to me very much like a sweet, precious bird, she naturally left this world, and fell asleep exactly as she had learned to live, directly and faithfully obeying the movement of life, with neither fuss nor argument.

Last night she came back to me; her presence so powerful that I was infused with an awareness of the archetypal Great Mother with her radiant power to foster transformation and rebirth. I awoke calling her name, Mama Carmela, Mama Carmela, Mama Carmela... and I remembered her healing touch!

Small Truth

The smallest thing
can enlighten
the path
illuminating the heart!

Verdad Pequeña

*La cosa mas pequeña
puede alumbrar
el camino
iluminando el Corazón!*

Dharma Poetry:

The Silent Presence

The silent presence within
is luminous
it allows every sound to emerge
it doesn't interfere with the mind
it is ever present,
embodying every word
and every sound,
holding us with tender care

It doesn't judge or demand
it only illuminates
our hearts
with the light of awareness.

La Presencia Silenciosa

La presencia del silencio interno
permite que todo sonido surja
no interfiere con la mente
es el eterno-presente,
encarnando en cada palabra
y en cada sonido
abrazándonos con tierno cuidado

No Juzga o demanda
y solo ilumina nuestros corazones
con la luz de la conciencia
.

The Secret Door

Are you not enraptured
by the tiniest wild flowers
that carpet the path
that you walk on,
or by the stirring sound of
water in a forgotten creek drying up
and evaporating into the sky?

Are you not enchanted
by the sound of geese
waking you up in the
early morning?

When we meet
we will cross through the secret
doorway
to rejoice about every little thing
we come across--
The new gray hair becomes
an unseen door opening
to another dimension
where only together we can go.
There we will discover
other small hidden doors
to cross through...
but only if we can find them first
in the deepest cave of our heart.
There...here...
we are the secret door.

Blossom of Love

I woke up early this morning
with a blossom of love in my heart,
touching every fiber in myself,
traveling through the sheets of my bed
to the trees outside.

All of them
the palm trees, the almonds,
the old and the new, just planted
the day before.

This love is resonating
as the sound of ocean waves,
splashing through myself.

And I surrendered to it
as a child or a newborn
simply allowing this Love to be,
what you are,
what I am
always available, latent and free,
to be given away
to rejoice every moment
when we meet as this love!

Hitchhiking

The unknown
is like hitchhiking on a desolate road:
You can't know
if anyone will pick you up

But in this uncertain future
you may find yourself
held and embraced
by all the space that surrounds you.

Its expanse can hold the tiny body
of your exposed self
in the middle of nowhere.

When you feel this embrace
no matter which direction
that you turn your face
you are in the hands of God
and nobody else!
The trees, the grass, the pavement
and the open sky are the same as you!

Trusting in the space that surrounds you
will arise within like a flower opening.

It will be made clear
with whom
to enter the car and *accept a ride*,
and your journey
is only beginning.

Mysterious Sender

Unexpectedly I got a gift today
from a mysterious sender
while the mind was embedded
in thoughts of human limitations,
the nature of this incarnation,
the penetrating pain of the body,
the imbalances inherent with aging
and the apparent ordinary life
of "less-than" wealth and resources.

This gift
opened itself without warning
and exclaimed,
"If one's true self is known
then there is neither birth
nor death, but eternal being-ness
and blissful consciousness"

In a moment this clear realization
exploded within and without,
liberating everything.

Clear seeing
became the invitation
to live in this mysterious,
fully-alive, always surprising
moment.
And the mysterious sender
is a silent embrace!

Dust in the Night

In this infinite universe
constantly full of events
suns birthing and dying
and galaxies hovering
with billions of stars...

I become like dust in the night,
witnessing
the unseen light of the day,
I travel far away beyond time,
bathe in luminescent light
and move in and out of the stars.
I am transparent
like the light.

In this unbounded universe
there is nothing that really dies.
It's a dance,
with forms and appearances changing
as if they die.

In this eternally alive cosmos
I am like dust in the night,
moving in and out of the stars

Joan R. Brady

MARTHA

A One-Act Play

J. R. Brady

ACKNOWLEDGEMENTS:

Winner with production in:

REDWOOD WRITERS COMPETITION
ONE-ACT PLAY FESTIVAL 2011

MENDOCINO PLAYWRIGHTING COMPETITION
ONE-ACT PLAY FESTIVAL 2011

SCENARIO:

A short riff on the life of Martha Mitchell.

Flashback to the 1970s - a story of love, betrayal and Watergate.

CHARACTERS:

JOURNALIST

MARTHA MITCHELL

JOHN MITCHELL

(Stage is bare. Spot lights JOURNALIST. He is fastening press pass to jacket.)

JOURNALIST

(To audience.)

Ah, there you are...my audience...allow me to introduce myself ...I am a journalist...a member of the press...an observer of life ...so to speak...and this gives me permission to go places most people aren't allowed...

(Beat.)

that is because I am recognized to be exact and impartial   although I have been known to improve my opinion in exchange for a good case of wine...a very good case of wine. I do have my standards...

(Beat.)

Mostly I cover the Washington circuit...Congress...the President ...big stuff. Been there a long time and I can tell you...it's not a world where people think much about integrity. It's more about what works...what keeps you where you want to be...except...once in awhile...someone comes along...

(Lights come up on MARTHA MITCHELL. She is middle-aged, flamboyantly dressed, with slingback spike heel shoes and bouffant blond hair.)

Ah...there she is...she's the one I wanted to tell you about...she was there back in my early years...back when I still believed I knew everything there was to know. Her name is Martha Mitchell...wife of John Mitchell...Attorney General to Richard Nixon...yes, that Nixon...another time, another place...

(Beat.)

Heroine, drunkard, madwoman...they called her many things. They still do...when they remember...but I'll tell you who she reminds me of...she reminds me of Cassandra...the most beautiful of the daughters of Hecuba...The way the story goes is...Apollo fell in love with her and gave her the power of prophecy...but when she spurned him he became angry and...since he could not take back his gift...he

decreed that forever more no one would ever believe anything that she said again...
>   (Beat.)
I suppose you could say Martha's situation was different...but still...

MARTHA MITCHELL
>   (Speaks with Southern accent.)
I was born Martha Elizabeth Beal, September second...mmmm...
>   (Pause.)

JOURNALIST
Born September second, 1918, Pine Bluff, Arkansas...

MARTHA MITCHELL
>   (To JOURNALIST.)
Ah...yes...thank you...
>   (To audience.)
My daddy was a cotton broker...he was a good man...but...

JOURNALIST
But...following financial difficulties, her father abandoned his family...
>   (Beat.)
when Martha was sixteen years old, he shot himself. She never spoke of it.

MARTHA MITCHELL
And why should I? I don't believe in dwelling on unpleasant things. It's not...well...it's not charming.

JOURNALIST
This lady was definitely Southern.

MARTHA MITCHELL
There were so many other lovely things to think about...and I was so popular...why there was the glee club...and the girls' cotillion

club...and the student council...I sang in the choir...I taught Sunday School. Oh no...I wasn't shy...not me...

JOURNALIST

In her high school yearbook, beneath her picture it says...

MARTHA MITCHELL

(Laughs)
About my voice..."I love its gentle warble/I love its gentle flow/I love to wind my tongue up/and I love to let it go"...I always did appreciate a good conversation.

JOURNALIST

In 1956, she met John Mitchell...
　　(Lights come up on JOHN MITCHELL. He is a balding middle-aged man dressed in a business suit. He stands facing audience. Throughout play he remains silent. Only his facial expressions change.)
At the time he was a successful New York attorney. A Colleague once said of him, "when you first meet him, he may seem cold on the surface...but that's only the tip of the iceberg."

MARTHA MITCHELL

(To JOHN MITCHELL.)
The first night we met you told me you would marry me. You said I would never have to worry about anything ever again. "Your problems are my problems," you said. I felt so warm...so taken care of.

JOURNALIST

At the time John Mitchell was married...but it was not long before he left his wife a note on the kitchen table and moved in with Martha.

MARTHA MITCHELL
We had the most perfect life anyone could have had. You would come home at night and we would sit together and drink martinis...and talk and talk and talk.

JOURNALIST
Always he would say to people, "isn't she beautiful?" And in her eyes...he was strong...he was handsome...he was wise.

MARTHA MITCHELL
I was so proud when you went into politics...especially when you started working for Richard Nixon. I knew he was the only man in this country who could truly save us from the Communists and liberals and welfare cheats...and from crime in the street and all that undesirable permissiveness. Oh you know what I mean...all those "hippy" people...they were so nasty.

JOURNALIST
When Richard Nixon was elected President in 1969, he appointed John Mitchell as his Attorney General.

MARTHA MITCHELL
Oh my...those were the days...weren't they, John? We knew Richard Nixon would lead our county back to the Right...back where we belonged...and he even said he wanted Cabinet wives to be involved...and maybe...one day there might even be a woman on the Supreme Court...and...best of all...best of all he said he had this secret plan to end that miserable war in Vietnam.

JOURNALIST
For some time, Martha had been advising friends to get their draft age sons across the border into Canada.

MARTHA MITCHELL

At first, I did like living in Washington. I loved to give parties   always with music and a theme. Political dinner parties were always the same. You could cover your eyes and know what the next course was going to be...

(Beat.)

Oh, I did know I didn't fit in because of the way I dressed...lots of color and high heels. But even if they were out of style men liked them...and I did speak my mind...

(Beat.)

Take desegregation for instance. I said it should have started right after the Civil War. But with all this stuff going on now...I don't see why they should just single out the South. What about the North? There's plenty going on there too...

(Beat.)

And all these people demonstrating...well it just shouldn't be allowed. Anytime you get people marching in the streets...it's catering to revolution. My family, they worked for everything they had...and now these jerks come along and want to give it all to the Communists. Why we're selling the United States right down the drain...that's what we're doing.

JOURNALIST

Initially...concern was expressed about Martha's "opinions"   but when her fan mail began to increase with each public statement...it was generally agreed, "she's the best thing we've got going for ourselves!" She was even given an office and staff to help her. They may have laughed at her...but they encouraged her too. She was honest...and people liked that   but then things started to change.

MARTHA MITCHELL

(To JOHN MITCHELL.)

I hardly saw you anymore. The President...he would call...day or night...and you would be gone. You know I don't like being left alone. I wanted to go back to New York. I wanted our life back   but you said

there was this thing we were creating that was bigger than we were...but you never really told me what it was   never...
>   *(Beat.)*

and what the President said about women being involved...he didn't really want us...not if we had our own ideas he didn't   and forget about putting a woman on the Supreme Court. It just wasn't going to happen...
>   *(Beat.)*

but the war...that was the worst. It just kept going on and on.
>   *(Beat.)*

What I did at that party...I know you said it was because I was drinking too much...but that wasn't the reason. I mean...when that General started telling those stories about how there were these young kids in Vietnam...teenagers...fighting against our American soldiers...well I just began sobbing. Don't you see...we had to get out. We had no business being there. I tell you it was a sad day when that man was ever elected. He was so concerned about getting his "enemies"...he didn't have time to think about the rest of us...not at all.

JOURNALIST
In 1972 John Mitchell resigned as Attorney General and took over the running of the Committee for Re-election of the President. Martha was booked for a rigorous schedule of public appearances...under close surveillance.

MARTHA MITCHELL
I wanted to be useful. I didn't want to embarrass my husband but I kept hearing things...seeing things...
>   *(To JOHN MITCHELL.)*

Okay, so I did listen in on your phone calls...and I did look through the things on your desk. I was afraid. As much as I wanted to believe you, I kept being more and more afraid. Then I saw the list, the outline for the "dirty tricks" you were going to use for the campaign...and there were those people from the teamsters that talked to you about how to handle things regarding Hoffa...and then that thing happened with

Muskie well it just made me sick...all of it did and I was afraid. I was afraid they were going to make a scapegoat out of you. I could see that...but you wouldn't listen.

JOURNALIST
So she started making late night phone calls...to me...to other people she knew...friends in the press. At first...no one took her seriously.

MARTHA MITCHELL
(To JOHN MITCHELL.)
For so long I did what I was asked to do. But then I had to tell someone that these things were happening...and they wouldn't believe me. They said I was crazy. You knew I wasn't crazy. You knew that. They said I had a drinking problem. Well we always drank our martinis together...we always did...and then you weren't here...and drinking the martinis reminded me of you and I wasn't so lonely anymore.
(Beat.)
They said I was stupid. "Look at the way she dresses...look at the way she does her hair...and those phone calls she makes...all those accusations...and that language...how could anyone ever take her seriously?"...and you goddamn you...you filthy stinking bastard...you heard them and you never said anything to help me...nothing. I was just trying to stop them...before more people were hurt. I wanted to stop them!

JOURNALIST
In the early morning hours of June 17, 1972, five men were arrested while removing parts of the ceiling from the sixth floor in the Democratic National Headquarters at the Watergate Hotel. With them, they had electronic equipment, cameras, walkie-talkies, and burglary tools. At the time, Martha was alone in Newport, California. Her husband had just left for Washington without her...
(Beat.)

What happened there was reported in a call she made four days later. Apparently she had tried to phone the press when she first heard about the Watergate break in...but was prevented from doing so....

(Phone rings. JOURNALIST mimes picking it up.)

Hello...

MARTHA MITCHELL

(Mimes speaking into phone. SHE is crying.)

I am sick and tired of politics. I gave John an ultimatum that I would leave him if he didn't get out. I am a political prisoner. All the time now there are people guarding me. Politics is nothing but a cops and robbers game. I know dirty things. I am not going to stand for all those dirty tricks that have been going on. I am sick and tired of the whole operation. When it happened...when those robbers did what they did...I tried to tell some one what I knew. I tried but they came at me...five of them ...and they pulled the phone off the wall and they threw me on the bed and they rolled me over and held me face down and they lifted up my dress and they pulled down my panties and then one of them stuck me with this hypodermic needle and the world...it just started to spin and spin and spin.

JOURNALIST

(Puts hand over phone. Speaks to audience.)

She said...when she woke up she was in New York City. She was in a hospital. There were bruises on her legs and thighs.

(Beat.)

Her statements were broadcast around the world. John Mitchell resigned from the Committee to Re-elect the President because "my wife needs me."

MARTHA MITCHELL

(Hand over phone. Speaks to audience.)

I had papers, documents from his files...things that proved what I said. I called the Special Prosecutor's office. I told them what I had but no one was interested...so I called this reporter from the Washington

Post and he came over and I gave them to him. He never said that I did that. I just wanted people to know. People had to know.
(Beat.)
Afterwards I was so afraid. I was afraid they were going to kill me...or commit me to an institution. After what happened in California I knew they could do anything they wanted to anybody. No one was safe...
(Speaks back into phone. JOURNALIST listens.)
Hello...yes...this is Martha Mitchell...about all those resignations and indictments...well let me tell you...if my husband actually knew about any of this stuff you can be sure Richard Nixon knew ...and I think he's the one who should resign for all he's done

JOURNALIST
(Hangs up phone. Speaks to audience.)
She made that call in 1972. It was more than a year later before everything that did happen happened...and the full impact of Watergate was upon us...
(Beat.)
As for Martha...her marriage was over and she returned to Arkansas. Occasional sightings reported her to be increasingly disheveled and bizarre. Three years later...she died of cancer at the age of fifty-seven.

MARTHA MITCHELL
(To JOHN MITCHELL.)
There was this dress I had once...the one I wore when we met the Queen. Do you remember? It was very full and made of these soft colored ribbons winding round and round...blending one into the other...and shoes dyed to match with very high heels...like you said you liked...and a big hat with flowers...and a parasol. I never felt as beautiful as I did that day...
(Beat.)
but they were upset with me because...when I was introduced to the Queen...I didn't curtsy. I mean, I don't think people should have to bow or curtsy to each other...and I said so....
(Beat.)

Oh they were mad at me for that...but you, John...you were so proud. Do you remember?

(Beat. JOHN MITCHELL caresses her face for a moment ...then turns abruptly and exits. SHE gazes after him.)

JOURNALIST
About Cassandra...myth says she predicted the fall of Troy. She recognized the Wooden Horse for what it was...but she was considered demented...so no one believed her...
> *(Beat.)*

At Martha's funeral...among the floral displays...there was this one all done up in white roses...spelling out in block letters "Martha Was Right." No one knew who sent it...
> *(Beat)*

but I can tell you this...it cost exactly the price of a good case of wine. So much for integrity...
> *(All lights dim out.)*

CURTAIN

For Jim Who Moved to Los Angeles

Poet man...lost and found in a city of angels...didn't anyone ever tell
you...to get to La Cienega and Sunset you need good freeway
directions
and at least...three sets of wings?

It's strictly a seraphim town...and if the cherubim forget their
diapers and arrows...they never make it to central casting.

And if you don't have a car you are left flat...on streets stretching from
Santa Monica to Pasadena...waiting for buses that run once every
three hours.

And no matter how long you wait...think twice before you get on
one...unless you
know who is driving...otherwise you might wind up some place
unimaginable.

Just ask the Black Dahlia. She'll tell you...if you can find her head.

It is all who you know...or say you know...and you did say you were
going to
shoot those videos and make those recordings...but something went
wrong and
word was you were almost homeless...and then you vanished...and we
thought
you were dead on a morgue table with a tag on your toe
saying..."Poet...DNA
determined...name unknown."

And then there you were again...found by that friend on a book tour....internet moment. Picture posted in a room sitting cross-legged on an unmade bed chanting,

"monkeys and sparrows...caught in the wind...nothing to lose...nothing to win...this is not a mask"

Form is tighter...more focused...but the vision has shifted. It's clear you're not in love with that girl from Chicago anymore...and sanity is a daily determination...but still...you do see horizons to wander into...if you squint.

And I do have some advice...because...you see...I was born down there in Angel Land...so I do happen to know a few things about it.

First of all...about that wing thing...you'll never fly if you don't try. It is all a matter of place...they say...at the right time.

Just remember...ultimately...all angels descend...so forget Icarus and think Pegasus. (As Roy Rogers used to say..."horse sense is the best sense.")

And...if you do make a crossroads bargain...insist on...at least...seven figures.

And if you ever do happen to move to Topanga...like you say you want to...be sure to keep your cats locked inside at night...otherwise...coyotes will eat them.

Pepin

Dance, dance, dance out of time...
There are no pictures of my great-grandfather.
He feared the camera would steal his soul, except
   for the wedding tintype my great-grandmother
   wanted so much, of them standing together against
   a pastoral painted screen, she, almost sixteen, in
   a borrowed white dress, he, stiffly suited, older
   by ten years, black hair wild about his face, and
   his eyes, the eyes that saw spirits, momentarily
   blinded by a flash of light.
I saw it once before it was misplaced by someone,
   long gone before me.

Dance, dance, dance out of time...
There are still fragments mentioned.
He was born mixed blood of French and Anishinaabe
   (Chippewa is a white name, a child divided between
   two minds. one of worlds' measured order, the other
   of circles, circles of the sun, circles of the moon,
   circles of the human heart, and which was which?
Mother? Father?
He must have told her back in the beginning, back
   when they still loved each other, and she did love
   him, the way an abandoned Irish orphan, raised by
   nuns, can love the first feel of freedom, and flesh
   and discovery of unimagined possibility.

Dance, dance, dance out of time...
The Anishinaabe say we possess two souls, one that
   travels in shadows and dreams, and one that stays
   deep inside the human heart, and if either is ever

lost, it leaves behind an emptiness, unendurable,
except when filled by wandering spirits who come
to warm themselves, then leave, without explanation,
and from the beginning there were spirits who came to
him and became him speaking an ancient language that
knew the cries of animals and of the earth and of
the wind.
And in the beginning she believed with him in
his voices of vanished worlds, for to her, Ireland
was a harsh distant world, and nuns knew nothing of
animals or the wind

Dance, dance, dance out of time...
The Anishinaabe tell a story of how a coyote, once,
fell in love with a star...but because a star
can never leave the sky, the coyote had to climb to
the top of a mountain so they could grab hold of
each other and soar together high up into the
heavens, where forever they could dance circling
the earth in an endless night.
But the coyote, being a thing of flesh and blood,
grew tired and numb and longed for sleep, and for
the sun, and, finally, it had to beg the star to stop
awhile, but the star couldn't because it was a star,
and so the coyote decided to let go and fall back
to earth, alone.

Dance, dance, dance out of time...
And I have heard it said that people can stop
loving for the same reasons they began.
New Orleans, St Paul, San Francisco...in the cities
the spirits, they stayed with him, holding him safe
against sadness, but never her, until their son died
and times grew hard and she railed against him
demanding a silence of voices that refused to know

her, and with whisky there came silence, and an illusion
of finding each other again...but then the space inside
him filled with such a darkness the silence became
all of him, and, even without whisky, there were no
spirits.

Dance, dance, dance out of time...
They say that when the coyote fell to earth it
   lost its first life but found a second that it
   lived less foolishly than before.
My great-grandmother remarried an Irish horse-collar
   maker who drank as full a measure as her first husband
   but, afterwards, would simply sing himself to sleep,
   and that was enough,
And no one ever asks about the star.
When my great-grandfather is remembered, always he
   is remembered for leaving.
It is supposed he died an alcoholic's death, anonymous
   in a Sacramento hotel room.
It is supposed but no on knows, and it is said that
   spirits of the dead wander forever in the circling
   winds looking for their own lost world, and it is said
   that blood runs thin through silence, dissolving time,
   dissolving memory, dissolving connection.

Dance, dance, dance out of time...
And always I have wondered about the star.
And when I look at our family album picture of
   my great-grandmother with her horse-collar maker,
   I feel their silences echoing inside me, and I
   know I almost understand the language of animals,
   and I know I am uncomfortable around cameras, and
   I know my own sadness always softens whenever I
   stop and listen to the wind.

Selkie

Through the boarded window, a ladder
   of light falls across frayed carpet flowers.

Candles burn low in red glass bowls...
   illuminating shadow mice, as they
      scurry from a dead cat's ghost.

Steel coils, spring up, ripping their way...slowly...
   through wine-stained, beige-velvet cushions.

A spider in her woven web...sits...
   suspended between wall and mandolin...waiting...
      as the handless clock ticks in time
         counted by a cuckoo's cry.

Forgotten food decays amid fragments of
   shattered porcelain...while the black phone
      rings over and over...
         then stops...unanswered.

Face up, a faded note lies upon the floor...

"Last night I dreamed of fuchsia fish swimming through air
   and when I woke, I longed, once again,
      to live beneath the sea...
         but I promise...I will be back often
            enough to water the gardenias."

John Field

Insomnia

While you sleep insomnia dehydrates
Each sip of your breath my parched ears drink.
A bus snores up our street
Plowing its headlights
Through our curtain.
"False dawn," the streetlights crow.
Why did you say no?

At midnight the tapping begins,
Softly at first,
Fleeting pains in my belly and chest,
Fear of death.
At two the tapping grows louder,
My heart thumping like a rat on speed
Banging a tiny tin drum.
If I had a knife I'd cut off its paws.

Three-thirty stretches and yawns,
Then veers away and disappears
Somewhere north of outer space.

At four I get out of bed,
Stand in front of the window
And stare at the moon,
A silver sleeping pill
Bathing the garden
In a soft decaffeinated glow.

Exhausted, I crawl back in bed
And feel your fingertips
Gently stroke my arm
Seconds before I fall asleep.

Remembering Chet Baker

'52 was the year Chet's junkie friends
Helped him forge a permanent relationship
Between his habit and his horn,
After which he spent the rest of his life
Filling empty spoons with his expensive muse
Whenever he felt out of sorts.

Neither awake nor asleep
When he walked on stage
Cool as a dead movie star,
He drove the ladies wild
With his wide and moony smile,
Pretty-boy voice
And lacquered helmet of slicked-back hair.
First thing he'd do
Was coax *Little Girl Blue*
Out of her cage—then paint the lyrics
Of her broken heart in dark and somber
Shades of gray, bruised colors he borrowed
From his long disease

Sometimes a girl in the front row
Would give him a *Let's Get Lost* look
Which helped him forget about
The needles in the alleys
And the fresh-dug graves
Long enough to consummate
Their telepathic love affair
With his microphone
By wringing a little honey
Out of *Sweet Lorraine,*
Something no other trumpet player
Could do, not even Miles.

In the '60s his career skipped a beat
Like somebody's bad heart
When a dealer he'd forgotten to pay
Kicked his picket teeth in.
Month after month after that
There were notes he couldn't quite reach
Because his dentures
Messed with his embouchure,

---Followed by nights
When the lights went out in his veins
Because the last vestige of his afternoon fix

Had dissolved into too much of nothing
In his blood, a problem he solved
By borrowing short term loans
From death
And sticking them in his arm.

Then safe in the certainty of oblivion
For an hour or two
He'd blow candlelight
Out of the shimmering flame in his horn.

Shroud *Mood Indigo* in an eerie neon glow.

Refract the aura of *Green Dolphin Street.*

And croon *My Funny Valentine*
As if it were the stuff of dreams
Instead of just a song.

Unless it was one of those gigs
When his tone was so full of troubles
It sounded like a commercial for suicide.

Friends who saw Chet
A week before he died
Said his face looked uninhabited,
Like something its owner had left behind
After he moved away.
They believe he accidentally
Fell out of his hotel window,
Only this time there wasn't
A featherbed of dope to land on.

Critics insist that he took his own life
Because reality finally outed
His inner nobody
And when he held his messy rendezvous
With a sidewalk in Amsterdam
There was no one left inside him
Death could kill.

Still Life With Snails

Great with peace of mind
After I hold a conference with a bottle of wine
I step outside into the noise-clear evening air
And with my flashlight switched on high beam
Stitch the sky's black nothing Into a canopy of golden seams.
Suddenly a nightshift of crickets rises out of the earth's scalp
Clicking castanets and tapping tambourines.
Their obscene cacophony stretches my patience
To the length of a fully expanded accordion
(((((((((((((((((((Or thereabouts))))))))))))))))))))))))
And in a bellowing voice
I order the tiny miscreants to knock it off.
Struck dumb by my godlike wrath
They instantly comply.

Duly honored by their silence
I stroll calmly through our garden
Like the second coming of the lord
Baptizing zinnias and hyacinths
With bloom-shaped blessings of consecrated light.
Tomorrow when their petals
Open to the morning sun
My wife will pick the prettiest ones
Unless a caravan of hungry snails
Inching its way in my direction
Gets there first.
Don't those creeping connoisseurs
Toting hotel rooms on their backs
Know who I am?
Perhaps they mistake me
For a soft-hearted New Testament deity
Or the garden's maitre d'.

Some of our neighbors melt them with salt.
Others suffocate them in plastic bags.
My wife crunches them under her heel,
Cleans up the result and doesn't flinch.
In the tool shed I pause for a moment
While I visualize my grandson's fragile skull
Smashed to a bloody pulp.
Then I put down my hammer
And honor my divine power
By not testing it a second time.

Sometimes Like Autumn

What is it about growing old?
Sometimes like autumn
Ascending toward its final glory,
The star of October's last picture show.
Begins with a gentle Rembrandt glow
Then erupts like ketchup and mustard
Splattered on buns, paint-box colors so hot
They shoot light off
To make themselves feel comfortable.
Stalled magnificence up there day after day
Until punctual as bad luck a storm sweeps in,
Trees shed their tattered gowns
Like nightclub strippers and the sky's confetti,
A sight that will open your pores
And make your shoulder blades ache for wings.

But it's not over yet:
Like soldiers in a defeated army
Left standing after their last salute
A few stubborn leaves crinkled brown
As powder burns
Refuse to come down
Because they can't decide
Whether or not they're still alive
And if so what for?
Then lose their grip on even this
And scuttle away on their rusty tips,
Turn epileptic in air
And with a lazy twirl spin silently down
Crazy-slow
Without a breeze to blow them,
Cashed in by gravity and finally run to ground.

"This is my life," you tell yourself,
"What old age is all about,
A drop of blood on a slide of glass
And death like a stone in my shoe."

Think about it. Take, if you like, all night
In the silence before the siren arrives
Because there will be mornings
When waking up in the same old pajamas
Just isn't enough----and nights that arrive
Like a coincidence instead of a sure thing.

Truck Stop, Jukebox, Jailhouse Rock

Wyoming, August 16th, 1977, heading west
On Interstate 80 trying to get some place real.
Behind me the amnesia of all those sad little towns
I've just passed through, way off in the distance
The Rockies and not much else around
Except a whole lot of breathing room.

Big sky country until dusk shuts it down,
Heaven and earth come together
In the nowhere out there and I tag along
Behind the glowing altar of my dashboard
With nothing better to do than feel instant empathy
For each infectious little bug
That measles my windshield.

Minutes, perhaps an hour later,
I switch on the radio and have its static in my ears
When a disc jockey informs me that Elvis is dead
Discovered unresponsive on his bathroom floor.
Let's go down, death said and he did,
Long live the king in stately quietude.
For a moment his face is a photograph
Pinned against the wrong side of my eyes,
His grin already history, an instant artifact.
Then the DJ plays "Heartbreak Hotel"
And what a sad feeling I have
When his voice comes back without him,
For goodness sake, from the underworld
Just below this one or wherever he's gone.

They'll open him up, I figure,
Because this has to be an inside job.
Then they'll say a few words at his funeral
And the next day Colonel Parker's traveling show
Will check out of Graceland and move on
To the next Podunk town with a hot itch
For its brand new ringmaster, his whip and his chair.
My thoughts blink at the glare, remember instead
The songs he sang on the Ed Sullivan Show
The night death touched his life so little
I believed his music would live forever.

Years later fame turned his mind into a balancing act
He kept falling off and turned his body into a spike
He pounded with pills instead of a hammer,
His mouth wide open for another one
Each time he stumbled around on the stage
Like a bloated Liberace imitator,
Spending and spending himself for his fans
As if there were no such thing as a reckoning.

About this time I can't tell
Which side of the white line I'm on
And need company fast
Because what a fever it is making do
With a few scraggly shrubs by the side of the road
And a scattering of bullet-blasted Burma Shave signs.
Wyoming, I love you! Bright lights ahead,
An all-night truck-stop with dozens of big rigs
Idling in its parking lot tidy in parallel rows.
Beneath a haze of cigarette smoke
I order coffee, a burger, basket of fries,
Slab of blueberry pie a-la mode.
Then I strike up a conversation with the fellow
Sitting next to me. "Did you hear the news?" I ask.
He makes a Sabbath of his face and nods his head.

After oblivion, guilty pleasure. Why not?
In the corner a jukebox holds its silence
Until my dime bails Elvis out of his cell.
Then it gets very excited as it lowers its tiny prick
Into the lyrics of "Jailhouse Rock"
And begins spinning the king's voice
Round and round on its haunted merry-go-round
Like a crazy Wurlitzer god making love to a ghost
While we sit at the counter, smoke Camels
And laugh at each other's jokes
The way good actors always do
To help us forget why we mourn.

First Kiss

Imagine the bare naked thrill
Of turning over a rock
And watching little white things
Writhe against each other in the dirt.
How did I get so snarled?
When I was fifteen I didn't know
How to do things with words
That knew what to say when I talked to a girl,
My thoughts either too shy or too weird
When I transferred them
From my mind to my mouth.

Night after night in a festival of heat
Between the sheets
I sighed and cried and cursed and prayed
That one day soon I'd discover
Love's true anatomy with Gretchen Glover.
Once I asked my older brother
What he and his girlfriend did
In the back seat of his Chevy.
His reply was a look which implied
That the drip in my personality
Was unfixable. So much for that.
Each time I measured myself against him
I got down on the ground and looked up at his knees.

Heart-jailed, I self-absorbed into myself
Like a worm in an apple, aware of the fact
That if I kept my feelings locked up
Without the possibility of parole
I'd end up babbling baby-talk.

At school my teachers
Needed documentary evidence
To prove I was alive.
Hour after hour I watched time's
Tired clocks tick-tock my classes away
Until they weren't anymore
And then took long solitary walks
Just to get lost
Instead of going anywhere.

Everything changed the afternoon
Gretchen shined her angelic smile
In my direction,
Detached my shadow's anchor from my shoes
And beamed me into the stratosphere.
The next day I took my brand new life
Out of its jewel box
And bought a pair of neon-green corduroy slacks
Loud enough to shatter glass.

Too shy—alas!—to fan my tail feathers
In front of her (afraid the older boys would laugh)
I strutted around like a showoff cock
Inside the castle walls of my previous life,
Perfect except for the fact that she wasn't there.

Worse still, I felt like a virginal medical student
Attending his first anatomy class
The night Gretchen and I
Watched Robert Mitchum chase Jane Russell
Halfway across Mexico in "His Kind of a Woman."

What could my sweetie possibly mean
When she whispered in my ear,
"Mitchum's got sleepy bedroom eyes
And so do you." How did she know
I hadn't slept a wink in a week
Worrying myself sick about our first date?

Seconds later she wasn't Daddy's little girl
When she gave me a tongue-tasting
Breath-sucking shuddering something
Akin to bliss. Maybe even LOVE?

Not so. Twelve hours later
My jukebox dreams ran out of nickels
When she fired her shotgun grin
Straight through me
And brought down the captain
Of the football team.

John Field

March Morning, 1944

Today I remember it all:
Sun running a mild temperature
Despite the calendar, a tired breeze
Searching for its second wind
And last week's snow
A slushy rash on the ground
Once but no longer white.

Above me God's huge blue
Wide open mouth
Munches angel-food cake
While a chorus of crows
In the choir loft of its singing tree
Recites hymns and proverbs.
"Believe! Believe! Believe!"
They squawk--and why would I not
On a morning so fine
That dogs leave their wags
Behind them.

Then nothing moves,
The world wonderfully perfectly
All to myself, accidentally happened on
Instead of sought,
Streets still as a photograph,
Nobody else out and about.

As I cross the West Side Bridge
The hard river beneath me
Lets out a groan
Each time a new crack appears
In its translucent skin.
Then gives up on winter altogether
And splits into the jagged pieces
Of a giant jigsaw puzzle
Which can't quite fit itself back together.

Amazing how a little violence
Settles the heart of a ten-year-old boy
Wandering his way through
The long unhurried diligence
Of his childhood.

John Field

The Natural Order of Things

When I was fifteen my faith unraveled to its core
for some reason I no longer remember.
That was the year I stopped begging
the earth's absentee landlord for an afterlife
and began paying close attention
to the natural order of things,
such as the graceful sight of songbirds in flight
before I blasted them out of the sky.

In July our valley turned into a landscape
of sudden vanishings when a flood
stampeded livestock and uprooted trees
down the Upper Iowa River.
On Main Street I watched men wearing hip boots
and dead smiles loot grocery stores
and then disappear in motor boats.
In our backyard the prehistoric stink
of rotting debris
outranked the fragrance of honeysuckle.

Deep in a daze that afternoon
and far beyond what I knew
I hiked the high-strung bluffs that circle our town
until I reached the sacred peak of Pulpit Rock
and then looked down into the angry heart
of a violent river. No answers there. Nothing. Never.
Just swamps where meadows used to be
and the kind of truth that's reserved for its victims.

So I looked up and watched a hawk
pause at the tip of its arc
and hang suspended in the air
as if welded there. Seconds later it broke free
from heaven's gravity
and slurred earthward in a liberating blur.
Then swooped up again so close to me
that I could see the tip of a tail
hanging out of its beak.
During that indelible moment
something shifted inside of me
like a drawer suddenly yanked open
and the contents of its secret compartment spilled out.
Later that afternoon I sold my shotgun to a friend.

John Field

My Tap Root

Each time I believe something is wrong
Or broken in my life because I made it so
My tap root stretches all the way back to Iowa
And the haunted house at the end of our block
With it doors kicked in and its eyes poked out
Then buries the tip of its guilty tail
Deep in the heart of the Midwest's bible belt,
The source of my lingering protestant guilt,
Not to mention the permanent home
Of my second childhood
Which I sometimes mistake for nostalgia's wall
I can just make out the barbed-wire top of
But never scale. Home, I dream of going home,
Lawns overtopped with trees
That wear their leaves like good-luck charms,

But when I arrive there
It's always winter by the clock,
Streets barbarous with ice, nose frozen
As I shovel out my snowed-in driveway
Then suddenly it's summer's annual disaster,
A brutal muggy August drought.
Listen! Everything is dry and still—so still
You can hear cars rusting in junkyards,
Clouds drifting overhead,
Puffs of wind granting dust-motes
Permission to live—then wake up and tell myself
I deserve better than the tricks
The changing seasons played on me
When I was a boy—and decide
That I want, I want, I want,
My hometown exactly where it is:
Three thousand miles away from me.

John Field

The Last Unicorn

born in an era when reality was a memory
forgotten in the blink of an eye
he was conceived in the womb
of a crazy poet's dream
then abandoned by his parents
because he didn't look right
his tiny cloven hooves just wouldn't do
and something else about him stood out in profile
which unnerved them
transcended the ordinary
and offered them little to hope for
and too much to cope with

heavy with a fading memory of home
he felt like a lost creature
lodged in his bones
as he roamed Europe's forests
the clop clop clop of its back-country roads
on mountains climbed slowly
and traveled easy and light
in Spain's olive groves
before he teamed up with a herd of wild horses
two-thirds stallion and one-third legend
he was truly a unique experience
for mares in heat

after he died historians
notorious for not checking their facts
declared him a myth
unworthy of even a footnote in the books they wrote
not so! artists claimed
as they wove his likeness into tapestries
where he still grazes today
in simulated habitats of flowers
and tall meadow grasses

Lucille Hamilton

Barking Dog

You can bark for all you want
but it won't scare off anything
I can see.
I think you know this, after all
these years of living here.

Is it that night's darkness doesn't show
you our property
the way the sunlight does,
so in the darkness beyond
there might just be…..
something?

I am right, aren't I, in thinking
you're out there each night
defending our home, or turf
might be a better expression?

Whatever it is you are doing,
please keep it short;
I'll have to deal with my nice neighbors –
in the morning.

The Ballgame

Every man, woman, and child was out for a good time.
The sun, the smell of the hot dogs - "and don't forget the *Guldens®*
and green relish."
There's this guy, sitting on the ground, doing yoga stretches, warming
up,
while flags of all colors whip about in the warm air and
dogs in funny costumes are paraded about in the name of some
cause,
who cares,
when the poodle's a convict in stripes,
the Chihuahua a politician in derby hat and cigar.
There might even have been a band playing. I don't remember,
what with all that was going on, the billboard entertaining with
flashing facts and colorful trivia, the boats in the bay tooting, and
seagulls whirling overhead.
A dad passing, knee by knee, carefully carries ice cream
for his very young son who wears a Big **A** on a shirt
much too big for him, sitting enthusiastically under a hat
that wears a Big **A** and swamps his happy face.
Everyone looks ahead at the field and talks sideways
yelling appreciation, roaring appreciation, then groans and laughter.
This is the arena of patience and swift judgment.
Our team lost, but you wouldn't know it.
We had such a good time.

We had a ball!

Crows

Crows have ink-walked
across the neat stack of
folded, white paper
I keep by my bed.

This means it will be a morning's dance
deciphering
what I've written down
in the dark of a late night before sleep.
Hopefully,
some worthwhile thought -
what the thought was
I just don't know.
It flew
right out the window
hours ago.

Dancing, Dalliance, Debarking, Delightful

Of course it was during the thirties. Boat cruises and all the wonderful send-offs with colorful streamers and champagne and boat whistling and tooting. Crowds were everywhere.

Turning back to our stateroom on the second deck, such a grand view of the bay broadening into ocean as the shoreline receded. Going down the Grand Staircase to lunch in the Grand Ballroom, the orchestra playing "Toot, Toot, Tootsie, Good-bye" and other lovely jazz nonsense. Everything was festive and gay, everyone was happy. Caviar, smoked oysters, you name it.

A brief nap. Henry, of course, up and about, *schmoozing*, I think the word is. He was never one to miss an opportunity, building up connections and sales. This was our first trip to the Far East. Henry has gotten it into his head that he could make a mint selling his *Rolls Royce* automobiles to what he called "the rich potentates of the East." So there we were, headed out for half a year of traveling, building up trade among the titled and the wealthy tea plantation owners.

He had seen to it that I had the latest *Chanel, Mainbocher,* and *Schaparelli,* while he stopped at his tailor's in the City to update his wardrobe. He even insisted that all my undergarments come from Italy and be of silk - which gave us both pleasure, I can assure you.

So we ate and danced our way through Suez. Well, you know from your own experience that from there on out, the weather is entirely different from home. No more dancing late what with the heat becoming the "topic du jour." Everything seems to sag after eleven in the morning. Too hot for morning tea, but great for Pimm's once the whatever it is has gone over the yardarm. Even Henry wilted, which made me relieved in one way that at least he was human like the rest of us, losing his usual crisp, take charge, full speed ahead.

We formed the habit of drinks in the bar, dinner and then chatting with others as the orchestra played each night in the ballroom. Although others were dancing, we simply found it too hot and stayed put, chatting away. I really wasn't interested in the conversation as Henry was, as always, still working, making contacts and being pumped-up cheerful, which almost everyone else seemed to find attractive.

I'd sit, stirring the watery drink, looking around the room, as were some of the other women at the table. I started to look at the details, the intricate woodworking of the stage and panels. It was then that I spotted the dark, handsome man playing the bass fiddle. He was a whizz with it, bringing out twists and tricky turns during his solos. We "twigged." Henry would be still working when the orchestra folded for the night. It was only the first time with the fiddler that I was late getting to bed. Once established, we found other times and places to meet which worked out well.

He was a good lover, and I began to fantasize about our life together. He said he wasn't married, coming from an extended family in Indonesia. He had no education to speak of, but once he'd gotten the job on board the ship, had started reading some of the great writers of Western literature on his time off. I know that he knew he was handsome, just the same way I knew that I'm an attractive woman, but, except for jokes between ourselves, this didn't matter. And I can't tell you how refreshing and clear this felt.

After Suez, the steamer made relentless stops at its ports of call: Singapore, Java, Sumatra, and so on. By the time we got to Indonesia, I had made up my mind; I would leave the ship and belongings in Java, disappearing to start a new life with my love, happily wearing sandals and colorful cotton batiks, fresh flowers in my hair and welcomed into an enormous, affectionate family, a new circle of friends, and the love of our long, good, simple life together.

As for Henry, he got over it in time, returning home with lots of sales and potential connections, which made him happy. He married Maud, his office secretary, who made him a good wife – happy to serve tea and drinks to his friends and potential customers. We kept in touch, occasionally visiting each other. All things forgiven. He even lent us money to get our own plantation which is now successful with the loan repaid with interest. Every once in a while, my man will get out the bass fiddle and I'll dance to his wild rendering of "Toot, toot, Tootsie" collapsing into his arms to watch the night stars splashed across the dark immensity of sky.

My man and I just love happy endings; that's what we work for, for everyone.

Two A's

In November the fog would roll in so thick you wouldn't know there was a river down there, at the bottom of the cliffs. The house was old, made of stone and big enough for the big families of that time. Although there were five children to split the property, only two were interested. The others wanted to move out into the nearby city. So the house went to Alice and Agnes. Alice was the elder by six years, and while this made for edginess between them in their younger years, this seemed to disappear over time.

They decided to share the house, dividing up the chores as well as the space. Agnes, who loved to cook and garden, took up weaving baskets, using the reeds from the river directly below the house. Alice, on the other hand, had always wanted to have sheep so she would be able to card and dye their wool into yarn for weaving. The two laughed, saying that maybe later they might open up a B&B. In a few years, Alice met Arthur and, after a honeymoon of sorts, he became a member of the household with the three getting along well. Also, he helped relieve Alice of the rounding up of the sheep, freeing her to have more time for her weaving for which she was becoming well known.

The days seemed to fall into a peaceful routine, Agnes out under the cliffs selecting reeds, Alice with her weaving and sheep, and Arthur helping Alice with her growing herd.

One night, Agnes broke an antique platter that was part of Alice's inheritance. It didn't seem important at the time, but it was. It opened up the whole festering inheritance issue: the "You got the painting you knew I always wanted and what's more you've taken it into your side of the house so I never see it anymore" sort of thing. It got so out of hand that they would sit at opposite ends of the table, passing food when requested, but never speaking. Their relationship, if possible, got even more ghastly. Things they had shared began to disappear into one or the other's part of the house. After some initial attempts to question these disappearances, nothing more was said. The level of resentment became hatred to the degree it was almost palpable.

It was after such a day in late November, that Alice, upstairs with the beginnings of a cold, asked Agnes if she would mind going with Arthur to help get the sheep into their pen. Agnes nodded her reply and put on her dark winter coat and shoes, before going out with Arthur into the foggy night.

Alice made herself nice, warm rum toddy and retired with a good book. It got late and later, and no signs of the two. Towards midnight, Alice heard something at the door and opened it to Arthur, but no Agnes. "Oh, good dog!" she said, "good dog!", welcoming the sheep dog in from the dark and petting the huge animal. "Oh Arthur, you're such a good herder, such a good, good herder."

Alice finished her toddy, folded her book and went to sleep, Arthur at her bedside. She phoned the police the next day to notify them that Agnes was missing.

Agnes was found two days later, dead among her beloved reeds. As there was no suggestion of a crime having been committed it never occurred to the police to think Arthur might have given Agnes a good shove off the cliff as wherever would a dog have gotten such an idea?

The following spring, having hired some help, Alice opened the house as a B&B, changing Agnes' old side into an exclusive apartment with a superb view of, and convenient to, a famous international city. The Tourist Bureau, on inspection, apologized for giving her only a double "A" rating, explaining that the third "A" could not be given as the B&B was not actually in the city.

Alice, on the other hand, couldn't have been happier. She chose to think the two "A"s stood simply for Alice and Arthur.

Silly

Silly is a great word,
when you're new in life and have been given
a drink that bubbles up your nose
if you hold the drink too close.

Silly works well with new things in general,
but take it up a decade or two,
and let's say you tell your best friend
that you're in love with George.

"George!" she yells,
over the clatter of coffee cups
at the cafe.
"George," she repeats, "You can't be.
You can't honestly be thinking of George.
Don't be silly!"

This is when the word can knock you sideways.

Sorrow

Sorrow, like a spent dandelion,
scatters its seeds with the wind,
settling in places
where it can hide
unnoticed,
as the days pass,
as time lightens.

You can wander some summer's day
out in the warm sun,
out in the delight of a meadow's tall grasses,
and suddenly
come upon one full-blown
and it will overwhelm you
with the sudden grief of
remembered happiness.

A Blues Song

Mama was wise;
she used to say,
"Pick your fights
very carefully."

Oh, don't go away, don't go away,
don't go away more than ever;
my heart and I couldn't stand it.
Mama was so wise.

Cloudless days and dusty roads;
issues forgotten still come to haunt.
Sleepless night and tossed-about sheets;
the well is deep with lonesome.

Oh, don't go away, don't go away.
Don't go away more than ever.
Mama was so wise.

The road goes on around the bend
and doubles back on itself again;
what was once familiar now seems new;
what was is never quite what it was;
change has that trick of behavior.

Oh, don't go away, don't go away.
Don't go away forever;
My heart and I couldn't stand it.
Now, I am so wise.

Lucille Hamilton

Romance in the Year 4000

My guy's a 4,000-year-old alien,
he's as spry as a goat on a spree.
He may look a bit odd to your eyes,
but he's my very own trans-galactic hon-ee.

My bonnie's abode is on the star Sirius,
so it means when he wants to see me,
he takes the night wind from his front door
and spins across our galaxy's vast sea.

The traffic out there is intense,
dodging meteors, asteroids and such,
but he's really an artful dodger,
always good to have in a clutch.

When it comes to helium dating,
my guy's most stellar at fusion,
believe me, and I have to tell you,
his flash is not an illusion.
(The earth shook!)

So when you look up into the night sky
what you see is no meteor shower,
what you are really seeing
are sparks from our galactic bower.

Here's a toast: To your future and to ours,
may it be lovely and loving as can be.
Our home will always welcome you.
Our address? On Sirius, YES, seriously!

Sassy Black Bird

Sassy Black Bird
marching down the street,
a one-bird parade of crow
out for his morning's surveillance
of his bird-dom,
being certain that every bird and being
knows that **This is My Territory**
and **You**
are here at my sufferance, my noblesse-obliging.
Crows don't need crown or scepter;
their attitude does the work for them.
There's a lot we could learn from crow.

Walter

You never really knew facts about what people call the essentials of life when you talked about Walter. He'd disappear, but nevertheless, talk would always come around to him in our conversations down over breakfast at Louie's. There'd be a quiet in the conversation, and then someone would say, "Do you remember the day when Walter ......" and so the stories would start.

One thing Walter was known for was his brown overalls. To anyone's knowledge, he wore them every day, no matter what the occasion. He was always neat as a pin, but always wearing those overalls. We had no idea if he had only one pair or if he'd bought out the whole lot from *Wilson's Emporium.* We thought he lived at the Wilson's out in their barn on the outskirts of town, but weren't sure about this.

One thing we did know was he had taken on that stray dog - same color as his overalls, and they looked after each other, just fine. See Walter, and there'd be the dog. Walter taught **the dog**, which was his name, to sing "Moon over Miami." Sing, of course is questionable, but they performed a duet on amateur night that was so successful, what with encores and all, that their act was repeated each year, even drawing out-of-towners who'd come specifically for their performance. After a number of years, the dog got tired of it all and began to sing off key. So Walter quit. And that was the end of that!

Kids didn't understand Walter and would play pranks on him. Once Walter, when he was at the Wilson's, was shaving himself with one of those old-fashioned strop razors. The bathroom had a chimney right near the sink where Walter was lathering up. The kids threw down a lighted firecracker which exploded just as Walter raised the razor to his cheek. He flew out at those kids, chicken-flapping mad, raising both arms and hell. They were so frightened into good behavior, the event pleased everyone in town.

He took up the harmonica in later years and joined *The Thumpers*, a mixed group of some old geezers and some of the young college kids. They could wrangle good melodies out through all their ramifications and then some.

As I said, after a while he just wasn't there - he and the dog just weren't seen again. Except on amateur night and on many other occasions when the heart longs for the good old days of honor, respect and fun, and then they see them again.

When the Cowboy Fell

When the cowboy fell off the barstool,
there was a rousing cheer;
another round was ordered,
and, believe me, it wasn't for beer.
We laid him out on a long table,
a candle at his head and his feet.
He must have been a "young-'un"
or he'd a-handled that tequila just neat.

The funeral was set for a Thursday,
but God had another plan:
That boy'd entered the bar as a young kid,
spirits saw that he left like a man.

The Dog That Looked at the Moon

Finn appeared in our lives one autumn afternoon when we were having a break from our chores, sitting out on the lawn overlooking the islands that have surfaced near in the bay of the mainland. They have taken on the aspect of the Arthurian tales of mystery, of places where the wounded spirit goes to be revived. And it is true, for I have seen just a casual tourist altered by a visit to the isles, experiencing a change that is quiet and yeasty in its ability to rise and form some self-questioning that leads to change and reassurance.

We had no idea where Finn, as we came to call him, came from. We were having tea and he just wandered up our slight hill and sat down, head on paws observing. He had no collar and as no one claimed him, he became ours. He came as a frolicking shoe-munching puppy, and grew into a thoughtful and intuitive being, able to watch with wisdom and affection the interplay of the humans he had taken on.

He could tell the shift in the weather, which can be quite sudden living among the islands as we do. He knew when and where fish were gathering and kept us informed of predators, barking at skunks and deer. He could read people's intentions. It wasn't until some time passed that we became aware of his many skills at understanding and translating for us that which is unseen.

The picture of him you have held in your hands, well, I'm sure you have felt the magic of it. There is a story that goes with it. Christine is an artist who lives further up the hill on the edge of the forest. She and her husband have lived on Barra all their lives and are familiar with the folk tales and myths such places hold to themselves. Christine has the same "eye" as Finn. They understand each other and it was she who taught us to pay proper attention to Finn and his behavior.

We all know how the moon affects us. It does so particularly with Finn. He will go down to the beach at the full moon and sit, sort of meditating on what that world traveler has to teach him. The effect on the tides, the running of the fish, foxes in the woods and the return of spirits for good or mischief. Finn "knew" that the Ferguson's calf was in danger alone in the woods, that Angus was having trouble with the haul of salmon he had landed, that Elsie's barn had caught fire. That sort of thing. He also anticipated events: if you found him sitting and not budging from some place, you'd better pay attention as something requiring your attention was bound to happen.

It has been a long time here on Barra since we've had a Spirit Dog with us and it is important to recognize that it has happened with the coming of Finn back to our island world. It encourages us and reminds us to pay attention to what is natural and nourishing to us and our world, that there are always signs out there for our interpretation. That is why we have come to sit beside Finn on nights when he is down at the beach watching the full moon rise in the sky, enlightening us all.

What Does It Matter

I was coming down stairs to explore a thought,
and realized that if I died at that moment,
the way I was dressed might entertain
the finders, the unlucky; compassionate ones
who have to deal with such matters.
Different bed socks - one has polka dots -
on my night's cool feet.

I am amazed at how the ego, pride
pops up still,
and started to laugh; my old nightshirt,
a souvenir a friend gave me, advertising
a fund-raising gospel-singing
concert in Harlem's Apollo theater
April of 1991.

I have a habit of folding down the page
of a catalog picturing something I'd like;
keeping the image of its pleasure
until the realization of what it costs,
where it would fit in my life
takes over and I toss it, getting on
with my life.

How can we balance our lives in a world
that has gone crazy.
It is in remembering pleasure, love,
a lot of intangible things among the real,
but always in the company of those
seeing amidst all the rubble,
a green stalk is rising.
We can deal with the rubble -
we have for generations -
it's the future of the plant
I'm concerned about.

Michael James

Before Winter Comes

To the old man in the rocking chair under a down comforter, the profound silence of the fading afternoon brought back memories of a time at the other end of his life when only the wealthy could afford the cost of quiet and peaceful retreats. Others had to put up with the noises of consumers, arrogant in the assumption that their wasteful lifestyles could continue indefinitely.

Today there was no sound other than the susurration of the sea breeze, tame on this clear day in early October, containing few scents, and carrying a chill it had rarely borne during the first decade of twenty-first century global warming. However, as traumatic as it had proved to be, the rapid warming had been short-lived in this part of the world. Everyone in England had been surprised by the speed of its fading, particularly the people who had studied in school the history of the glacial periods and of variations in earth's climate. There had been rapid climate changes in the past such as those that occurred 11,000 years ago, but nothing like the changes that had brought on the prolonged warm period, then suddenly ended it in Northern Europe.

Gordon Heatherton had been making kindling wood by splitting short pieces of fir. He could peel off pieces one growth ring thick like a chef making celery sticks for very small people, his cleaver rising and falling in rapid succession that told of his still firm grip and his concentration. Now he wanted to bask in what was left of the sun's rays and let his eyes rest on the distant undulating landscape as it fell gently towards the sea that formed the horizon, stretched across his vision in a more or less straight line.

The river, winding through the folded land, glinted here and there where the westering sun was reflected as if someone had struck arcs for tiny lamps. And as the sun moved, the lights winked out then came on further downstream. On clear days he loved seeing the red orb slide into the sea and sometimes couldn't help wondering if parents still told their curious children how the light was extinguished by the water only to be miraculously rekindled the following morning. But he suspected few watched sunsets any longer, and fewer thought in terms of miracles. However, something in the order of a miracle was going to be needed if his son and his two boys were going to arrive safely in Marseille for the trip to the warm lands across the Mediterranean.

In Gordon's boyhood in the village, down a thread of a road as remote as anything could be in Dorset, there used to be very few seconds of silence between man-made sounds that intruded themselves into one's consciousness all day long. The beep of a video-phone, the whir of wind generators, children's voices in play or argument, were part of the normal background. Now he waited in silence in the afternoon sun for the crunch of rubber tires forcing little rocks against each other to announce the arrival of his son and two grandchildren.

At last the excited voices of children, then the repeated ringing of their bells announced their presence before Gordon could see them pedaling slowly up the path, each bike with its trailer of precious possessions in tow. He'd been expecting them any day now and was eager to see them. He threw off the comforter and stood up a little stiffly, using the handrail to negotiate the porch steps. It wasn't only his infirmity that kept Gordon from striding down the steps; his level of energy was not as high as it used to be when there were more calories in his diet.

The two youngsters, who had sprinted along the flat before the house, dismounted gingerly, stretching their legs, and rubbing sore backsides. The younger was full of information and chatter. "It's warmer here than at home, Grandpa," said Tom, as he squatted to ease his muscles. "Can we go fishing tomorrow?" When he rose he hugged his grandfather quickly; his brother gave the old man a longer hug in silence, a slightly rueful look on his face. Though he smiled, he was obviously in pain.

"There's hot water ready for you two," offered Gordon to his grandsons. Then, "Go soak those sore legs!" As they hobbled into the house, he watched his son get out of his bike and close the plastic canopy. The younger man shook out his legs as if they were trousers, and pulled his father to him with wide open arms. Both were watery-eyed while his son patted the old man's back reassuringly.

"Have a good trip?" inquired Gordon stretching his arms so he could look into his son's eyes.

"Pretty good, Dad," he replied. "Couldn't find much to eat on the last leg of the trip, though. Sure hope you've got enough here!"

"I do, Son. The fish have been plentiful, and people have left crops and cattle in the fields. How were things looking in the Midlands when you went through?"

"Empty," was the single word reply. His son paused. "There's a big difference since I came last May. Junk all over the place; not much sign of people working; very few places to eat and those only carrying local harvest food. No long haulers. There were farm tractors on the roads, a few motorcycles, and of course, bicycles. What did you think of that long line of bikes I showed you yesterday on the phone?"

"They looked pretty ragged. Must have been on the road for weeks." Gordon paused. "Son, it would have been a tough winter for you this year up north. Who's running the show now that the department is closed down?"

"A bad lot of vigilante hoodlums!" answered Dan disgustedly. "They have no more idea of how to run a country than I'd know how to run a school. It's all over up there." His father nodded gravely.

"But Dad, there's something I wanted to tell you, though not over the air 'cause of the snoopers. It's really good news. Our whole constabulary has been offered jobs by the Displaced Persons Authority in Algiers to help supervise the British camp outside Tobruk.

"So that's where Di has gone!" exclaimed Gordon, smiling. "And that's where you're headed."

"DPA figured since our men had worked together, they'd hire us as a team. One of our guys who has been keeping up with climate changes for years worked it out in advance as soon as he saw which way the chips would fall. They want us to come down and join their guys with whatever of our equipment we can bring. Everyone's on his own, but they sent us rail passes that include our bikes. All the heavy stuff is there already, and the women and small children. We're going to bivouac with the DPA at the army museum where they keep the relics of Rommel's and Monty's armies from WW II, which is still fenced. It's been in the hands of their National Guard for years. Now they've been telling our people the old barracks have been repaired and converted to family housing. They are almost ready for us now. We're going to live and work right out of them."

"D'you know what they're like?"

"Di showed them to me as if she was just panning the local scenery, then dipped her phone over the one we'll be in. It's three stories high, concrete block with small windows and well inside the fence."

His father whistled. "You're landing on your feet again! And of course, Tobruk's on the railroad, if I remember. Across the railroad is a highway, then the sand dunes and the beach. How did you say you fell into that one?"

"One of our deputies who had actually been down there as a sort of premature task force heard about the riots in Marseilles and got hold of his contact again. DPA jumped at the idea of acquiring a whole crew.

"And how about the town? Is there still a military base as well as a museum?" asked Gordon.

Dan was reassuring. "Yes. They're next to each other. You have to go through the base to get to the museum and there's only one way into the base. It's gated and guarded. The base perimeter fence is patrolled twenty-four seven. I think it's going to be headquarters and living quarters for the Guard as well as DPA law enforcement." They both understood the need for security given the floods of refugees from the north and the mountains. Logistics were already nightmarish: totally insufficient housing, transport, food, water, and sewage.

The children had been listening in the doorway to their bedroom, and the older boy, Nicky, a serious fourteen-year-old, addressed his father. "Dad, Tobruk sounds like some sort of prison. I mean, living in barracks inside an old army base, guards day and night? For real? Will we be allowed out?"

Quietly his father answered him, "Nicky, you may not want to go beyond the fence when you know what's out there. You saw those vigilantes we passed on the way down. If there'd been fewer families in our caravan d'you think they would have let us go by without trying something? They surely knew someone in such a large group would be armed. And those guys were tame compared to what's going to be prowling around outside the fence in Tobruk."

"So we're going to a war zone?" the boy asked.

"From what I can find out, probably something like that though those kinds of people will be outnumbered. There will be officers like me keeping the peace." His father looked him straight in the eyes, nodding his head slightly. "The hard thing is going to be getting there. I've a feeling we have a difficult road ahead unless we're lucky enough to be allowed on the train when it gets to Tobruk."

"Why wouldn't we?" asked Tom, his other son. "We have passes."

"I imagine, so do hundreds of others," answered his father. "And even if we get on, will they let the bikes on too? If they don't, how will we get around at the other end? We just don't know. You saw how it was for your mom with all those people milling around when she was trying to get from the train depot to the Fort and held her phone above her head. But you heard her. Didn't she sound relieved that we'd be getting a safe place to live?"

His sons both nodded while Nicky looked quickly from his father to his granddad. The adults wore expressions that gave nothing away.

"Let's go in and have a bite to eat," urged Gordon breaking the silence. "Your lot must be hungry and there's delicious smoked salmon and mashed potatoes and carrot and chard waiting for us. The stove's roaring and it'll only take ten minutes for dinner to be ready."

The old man shepherded the family toward the dining room knowing that the fresh food would be a treat for them all.

There was not much to stand between a full belly and a bed for the saddle-sore, weary children and they were out cold before the dishes were washed. Father and son would have a little time to share.

"Dad, you know we'd like you to come with us, don't you?" asked Dan when they had settled into armchairs.

"Yes, son, I think I do, and I thank you. But you know that's out of the question for me. We've discussed it often enough; nothing's changed." There was an embarrassed pause. Soon Dan took up the thread of conversation again.

"How's the net working?"

"Great! Everyone's on line at all times with these," answered his father pointing to his mike-headset. "'We're the greatest bunch of chatterboxes you've ever heard."

"And the power grid?" asked Dan casually.

"So far so good," was the reply. "We're all generating one way or another and our capacity far exceeds expected needs and all emergencies we've had. In fact there's a start-up grid up the coast that's going to join ours until their generators put out what they need. We're going to export microwave power! How long's it been since anyone's done that?"

"I dunno," came the laconic response. "We never got into that because of the hydro. But of course that's history; with the lakes and streams frozen there's no more running water so no generation. We were spoilt!"

"We all were," agreed his father. "Now it's only the wind generators that put out anything worthwhile, though you will have plenty of solar off down south, right?" His son had tuned him out and responded with a non sequitur.

"Di said you'd be allowed to live with us in the barracks. She checked."

"Well that's great, son, but I'd be a burden to you as I became less able to take care of myself. Your family will be restricted enough as it is living in those crowded camps facing thousands of people camped like ants all over the countryside and looking for shelter and food. I couldn't face that. Only the strong will survive down there; we've seen that here already when the refugees from Norway came through. Apparently they were at each other's throats as soon as they started south.

"I sure understand what you mean, Dad. If I were on my own I would stay here too."

"Not at your age, son. You have too much vigor to face a slow death through cold and hunger."

"What about the fish? You said yourself there was a good run of salmon this fall."

"There was, indeed. But that was because we had more rain than snow this year and the river is running full. It won't last; we all know that. When the headwaters freeze, the river will dry up and the salmon will stop coming. It's just a matter of time. Remember what it was like three years ago? That was a lean time." There was a frown between the old man's eyebrows as he paused in thought.

"Dad, I hate the thought of you being unable to bring in enough wood for the stove and freezing to death in bed, or slipping on the ice and breaking a hip. And even if these things don't happen, even if a neighbor comes to help after a fall, you'll eventually starve to death." There was pain in his son's voice and the sort of quiet intensity you hear when a friend is trying to persuade an ill person to agree to some radical and dubious procedure.

"All probabilities," admitted his father with a rueful smile. "'But would I rather be trampled by a mob in an over-crowded valley where the authorities have to store the sewage in lakes because they haven't been able to build treatment plants fast enough to meet the influx of people fleeing the cold and where armed men and dogs guard electrified fences around anything containing food? I don't think so."

"But Dad, climatologists are saying the weather might get warm again like it did this year."

"Son, I've tried to explain it to you: any warming will be a temporary and maybe a local event bucking the trend. We might have mini-warming or further cooling periods in which the temperature rises or falls by a few degrees like the global warming we went through at the beginning of the century, which of course, was man-made. But the overall change is toward a cooler climate and that's what we're seeing happen. You know as well as I that it only takes a worldwide average temperature drop of six degrees to plunge us into another ice age. That's where we're headed. The greenhouse effect stalled it for a while but it couldn't hold back the inevitable." He paused and leaned back in his chair. "A number of brave climatologists warned us some years back not to get our hopes up about warming as a permanent phenomenon. And here we are." He looked at his son with sad, resigned eyes. "We have to make the best of it, which is what we've all been doing, right?"

Dan looked into the stove whose embers were all aglow. His face reflected its fiery light. "I've really missed you and the talks we used to have, though they never seemed long enough to say all I wanted to, and now how much time do we have left together, Dad?"

"Well, you know your schedule better than I do, but don't you have to be at the ferry on a certain day?"

"We can stay here for two nights, no more."

"Then let's make the time count," responded his father. Father and son hugged and went to their bedrooms without showing each other their faces.

On their only full day together, the adults rose before the children and went for a stroll on the beach; it was wider than Dan remembered it to have been. That would be due, he knew, without his father reminding him, to the increase in precipitation as snow, and to its build-up on the mountains of the interior. They chatted about the distant past when the man was still a carefree boy with his whole life ahead of him, when what he wanted most of all was to be a football star on the high school team.

"When I refused to sign the papers for you to play football because of the injuries I'd seen players suffer, and because of your dislocated knee, what effect did it have on you that I didn't see?"

"That's a harder question to answer than it seems," replied his son. "Can you stand the bald truth?"

Instead of answering, his father said, "I imagine you hated me for it, that you felt I was arbitrarily preventing you from realizing your dream. I think now that your unwillingness to give college a real try and to develop yourself intellectually may have been your way of showing me how wrong I'd been to deny you your sport."

"Something like that," answered Dan. "Though I don't think I reduced my feelings to that kind of a tit for tat. I knew you thought you were doing it for my own good, but I certainly didn't see it that way. What really got to me was your certainty that you were doing the right thing. You were so damn sure you were right that I couldn't begin to try to persuade you to change your mind. And Mom didn't try either, at least not hard enough." There was a long silence as the two men made their way over the sand.

"Do you remember when the resentment began to fade?"

"It gradually wore off after I left home, after you did some nice things like crating up my bike and sending it to me. But the really big change came when you attended my graduation from the Academy and I understood you to be proud of me, as I was too. That was when I started to appreciate and love you as an adult." They stopped walking and turned towards each other. "Then came the time of trouble when you and Mom stood by us till we got through it. That put everything into perspective once and for all time."

"You know, son, when I started to get frail and really felt my age, I was also able to feel your love more fully. I want you to go away from here knowing that your love has lit up my life for years. Even across miles of countryside, it has been the warmest and dearest part of my old age. Now across the sea and in another nation, I'd like you to feel my love for you a constant in your heart."

"I shall, Dad. You'll never know how much your love has meant to me. It has been something I can always come back to when times get tough and I'm sure it will be there for me always."

"Thank you, Son. Now let's go make breakfast for us all."

To the old man in the deck chair at the edge of the beach, his son and grandchildren were already three black specks as they pedaled along the flat sand exposed by the ebbing tide. He couldn't distinguish one boy from the other even with his binoculars, though his son still stood out by his larger size. In thirty minutes he expected them to round the headland on the south side of the long bay.

He felt strangely at peace after the upset and pains of farewell. His son had sobbed with abandon, and the old man had been almost as bad as they faced the reality of never seeing each other again, and of the likelihood of not even being able to communicate. Now it was over; his family was disappearing fast and he was determined to let the image of their trek along the beach burn into his brain so that he would have access to it as long as he lived.

That was not likely to be very long. He had kept the information of his terminal illness from his family lest they risk missing their ferry by staying longer with him out of sympathy. Now he had to face it alone: he was sick; his weakness was coming from within his body, most likely from his pancreas, he had decided a month ago.

Gordon put his binoculars to his face reaching out with his eyes for the last time to the three remaining members of his family, mere black figures against the almost white background of the sand. They seemed to be going seaward as they approached the headland. In a few minutes they were going over the last stretch of beach he could see; then they were gone. He put down his glasses, having nothing more to look at, and sat back to watch the play of clouds over the water.

All at once a dark speck came into view halfway to the headland from where he sat, and his heart missed a beat as a rush of adrenaline burst into his blood stream. Was one of them coming back, unable to leave the old man by himself? He fervently hoped not. He picked up his glasses and trained them on the object. It appeared to be moving rapidly and purposefully, though not as smoothly as a bike would travel over that sand. He removed his glasses to see if he could judge its distance with the naked eye and concluded it was about two and a half miles away and moving at too fast a pace for a person walking.

Another ten minutes and his glasses picked out the quartering run typical of a dog whose back feet would get in the way of his front ones if they tracked directly in line. Ten minutes more and the dog was black, had a tail, and was definitely headed his way. He would welcome a new friend with open arms, dried filet of salmon, and fresh water, and only hoped it wouldn't prove to be a Faustian bargain, a small black dog turning into Mephistopheles behind his wood stove.

He needed no surprises. To be sure, he determined to scratch a large pentagram in the sand in front of his door.

When the dog got within hailing distance, the watcher recognized it to be an emaciated border collie; he called out in what he thought to be a kindly voice, but the collie kept its distance and sat down on the beach panting. The old man got up and walked into his house to fetch provisions which he placed in front of the animal then retired to his chair. Once more he relaxed and watched the catspaws race across the bay, pushing little wave fronts before them on the water. He reflected how many times he had watched their performance from his sailboat, judging their likely impact on his sails by the height of the wavelets they produced and by their speed across the bay. He had always marveled at the blue-black color of the sea behind the catspaws contrasted to the almost grey blue it sported in front of them.

Out of the corner of his eye Gordon observed his new companion stretch over the water bowl before him and start lapping it vigorously. His thirst apparently quenched for the time being, the dog turned to the salmon and sniffed it cautiously. Finally satisfied it wouldn't eat him, he tasted it; then, in the blink of an eye, he had wolfed down the whole filet. Gordon hoped his removal of bones had been thorough. After his meal, the collie backed away from the man and sat observing him from twenty-five feet away. Their acquaintance was likely to be some time developing, thought his host, who knew how slow collies were to make new friends.

When night came on it brought a change in the direction and temperature of the wind, which was now offshore. The man could feel its mountainous origins, dry and cool. He thought maybe the dog would come inside later on and appreciate some shelter and warmth. He would make a fire and lay out a bed for the animal, begin the process of making friends again; it might help to fill the void in his heart.

A Courthouse of Fowls

A cousin from England is staying with me for a few days. Today I took him to the coast, straight to Bodega Headland, where we had difficulty holding open our car doors against the thrust of a 35-knot blast from the northwest. Hunkered down beneath the logs supported on concrete blocks to prevent cars from rolling over the cliff edge, two ravens eyed our approach as if measuring our auras for colors denoting our generosity. My cousin marked the particular insecurity of the lesser bird, how it seemed to defer to its companion as if to an older brother. I took out of my backpack a couple of good chips and walked gently up to the birds holding out my offering. As soon as they became uneasy, I flicked one under the log where it was immediately seized by the older animal, snapped in half, and the hard, jagged pieces swallowed one half at a time without a blink of the steady black eyes.

Cousin and I hiked up and over the headland, staying a little away from the cliff edge in case a gust of wind were to pick up my tottering steps and throw them over. It was hard sledding for this old bod and I was happy enough to sit on the ground and wait for his return, enjoying the silver sheen of the sun flickering on the waves as they rolled down from the north to crash onto the rocks below.

When we returned to the car, I observed how pleasant it was to get in out of the wind; much as I love it, one tires of it when it is so strong and steady. I suggested we drive down off the headland to seek a more sheltered spot for lunch. The bay was much calmer than the top of Bodega Head, and we found a picnic table immediately. A few gulls, standing or lying around the table, notified us of their presence and great need as soon as we sat down by opening their beaks wide and screeching at us in falsetto mode. My requests for quiet being soon observed, I opened our lunch bag and laid out the victuals and drinks. A circle immediately formed around us as if we were guests in their courthouse whom they welcomed with much raucous cawing.

I spoke to a few of the gulls near me urging them to shut their beaks if they wanted some scraps; two complied at once, a lovely mature bird with brilliant white plumage, trimmed in black, a white and yellow beak sporting an orange spot near its tip, and another bird dressed in the usual drab brown feathers and black beak of immaturity. I tossed scraps of my tuna fish sandwich to them, one at a time, apparently convincing them of my harmlessness, for they hopped up on the seat of the picnic table to retrieve scraps from the tabletop. And it wasn't long before both of them became bold enough to get up on the table itself, from where they then had to ward off flock mates diving in for treats.

Feeding seagulls in the past had convinced me to be wary of those beaks of theirs, for the top part carries a pointed hook which can pierce the skin of a finger tip with ease, not intentionally, but just because the birds strike to catch their prey like a snake darting out of its coiled position.

So I addressed my feathered new friend much as I have spoken to dogs looking for treats. I told the bird in a friendly, calm voice to take it easy, not to snatch, and that it would have seconds if it took the food gently. Then breaking off a little piece of my sandwich and holding it between thumb and forefinger, I stretched out my arm towards the animal and held it there.

The bird did a little foot shuffling, all the while looking at me with those passionless, unblinking eyes, black of pupil, yellow of iris, moving closer to my extended hand, withdrawing a moment, moving feet. Then all at once the gull committed itself and moved smoothly and gently to take the morsel from my fingers without even touching them with its beak.

"Good job!" I told it, and broke off another piece, this time with some tuna fish on it. The same little dance occurred, though not as long, and a similar easy retrieval of the snack took place, leaving my fingers intact. I was elated! Junior moved in to pick up little pieces dropped from the catch. So I tried to coax him into a civilized feeding too. He wasn't such a quick learner or quite as brave. I had to flick pieces to him, though he was still on the table.

The feeding continued until my sandwich was consumed, though admittedly mostly by myself, the walking having given me a good appetite. But I still had chips and an apple, though I could not imagine a bird being able to consume chunks of that firm fruit. Both tried; however their bills had insufficient leverage to reduce the pieces to pulp so they could swallow them. The chips they broke into manageable morsels demonstrating the use of their beaks as tearing and pecking tools. And when the remaining chips were only in small pieces, the gulls bent their necks so that the sides of their beaks were flush with the table. There I noticed slight bulges on either side, perfect for scooping up crumbs.

Like raptors, the eyes of Jonathan Livingston were almost in the front of his head, providing him over 200 degrees of vision and giving him that peculiar appearance of a hard stare. I was left wondering if it was this determined and hypnotic look that had separated me from my lunch.

As I sat there staring back at the bird, Jonathan Livingston seemed to place a query in my mind.

"Besides their usefulness for binocular vision, why do you suppose we have two eyes"?

"I can't imagine," I answered perplexed.

"So that we can look at the finger pointing to the moon with one, and at the moon with the other." With that he spread his wings, caught the wind, and sailed straight up into the sky which was too bright for me to follow him.

Tintagel

I expected crumbling ruins clinging to a cliff overlooking fierce Atlantic waves crashing on rocks. There would be "atmosphere," possibly even a drama in the scenery. The myths perpetuated by Geoffrey of Monmouth would play no part in my appreciation of place. As far as I knew, Arthur, a 4th century Celtic tribal chief trying to unite other Romanized Celts quarreling in the vacuum left by the collapsing empire, had never been near Tintagel. He'd been far too busy in central southern England to isolate himself on a remote western headland. And the castle originated in an era as remote from the 4th century as from our own.

So, as Janneke and I, conducted by Sid and Diana, walked down a fairly steep path next to a stream on the way from the village to the "castle" of Tintagel, Arthurian lore was not on my mind. I was thinking that the day was perfect for our visit; I was delighted to move into the sea fog that swirled around rocks and cliffs ahead of me, now obscuring much, now offering tantalizing views of what could have been chasms or caves. The blurring of things visible, which matched the confusion of history and mythology, would provide room for imagination if that were to take off.

As we neared the end of the downward path, space seemed to suddenly enlarge. Up became higher; down became deeper, further away. A huge headland towered over us on the left. A cliff face lay before us over which the stream poured itself through curtains of brilliant green moss and ferns. A steep flight of rock-hewn steps to our right led down to a small beach squeezed between a black promontory and the headland. Two enormous caves burrowed into the neck of the headland, their interiors swallowed by the dark inside. One could easily imagine a boat landing on that beach protected by the headland on one side and the promontory on the other. But as I looked for a passage for that boat, I could see it would have to negotiate dangerous rocks under water. It would have to be a landing at high tide.

As my eyes swept up the cliff face above the caves, I could see old stonework, ramparts, fortifications, arches high up on the headland. There were people struggling up a staircase cut into the rock, whose individual steps looked half as tall as they. Above them an archway in the old building formed an entrance to what must have been the main part of the castle.

The bottom of the staircase was fed by an upward-bowed, laminated wooden bridge that began at the end of another flight of steps on the land side of the isthmus, and sprang across a chasm separating it from the castle proper. The fort on the land side was protected by sheer cliffs on two sides and high walls, or their remains, on the others.

Janneke and I looked at each other, walking sticks in hand, then looked up at the rock staircase leading into the clouds. Sid and Diana retired, perhaps not wanting to embarrass us if we couldn't face the climb, perhaps not wanting to face it themselves.

"Come on, Janneke," I urged. "We can do it!" She grinned gamely, we waved goodbye to the others, and began our ascent.

At first the steps were just strenuous, and crossing the bridge gave us a chance to rest and look back the way we had come. Already we could see the cliff face where the stream went over at the end of the path, now showing its true shape, as a fall of water, and I thought of a woman who had lain down on top of the rocks and let her long hair fall over the edge. "Water tresses," I would have called the sight.

People passed us on the bridge, then waited at the foot of the staircase to allow others, nearing the end of the descent, to pass them. We would have to do that several times on our way up. Then we clung to the handrail, pushed on our sticks, and hoisted ourselves up one giant step at a time. With the steps so huge, I thought, it must have been exhausting for people to carry up provisions, not to mention fuel and water. And it was impossible to think of an attempt to mount an assault against the castle up that staircase.

After several rests and pauses to let others by, Janneke and I gained the end of the staircase, passed through the Norman archway at the top, which certainly dated the structure, and found ourselves in the main body of the old castle on relatively flat ground. Sea fog parted so we could see the beach below and the place where we had stopped to look about. Janneke thought she recognized Diana and Sid. We pressed on, looking at foundations of chapel, rooms, halls, then leaving through a rounded arch, to climb higher still, though now on grass.

Scattered over the fairly flat top of this headland were the remains of its former tenants: a walled garden, a man-made cave thought to have been used for cold storage, dwellings outlined by their foundations. We passed many of them as we walked towards the western edge of the headland. There great slabs of rock jutted into thin air over the Atlantic shining below through the fog. I sat on one of them to gaze at the ocean far below. Janneke, not liking heights, stayed back from the edge.

The sun, an obscure luminescence behind pearly white clouds, achieved no dominance over the landscape and cast no shadows. The sea was partially hidden by the fog. When patches of it became visible, lit up by the watery sunlight, I became a landlocked lady awaiting sight of the ship returning with her lover or Tintagel's lord expecting messages from a foreign shore. The sea didn't dominate either, though it mesmerized me in its gentle heaving and northern glimmer.

The shelves of stone jutting from the western cliff-top were like wafers, a holy eucharist in an earth priest's hand waiting to be accepted by an airy supplicant's mouth. The land itself was tenuous, suspended in air and in time as if awaiting a final resolution that gravity would decide. At this place on the isthmus, even rock didn't dominate the scene.

It was the air, which not only included, but which gave birth to land, sea, and light as if in artistic outpouring, that dominated the scene. I became aware, as never before, of existing in space rather than on a flat rock. That was Tintagel's first gift to me, the experience of space all around as if I had been inducted into the secret of my air sign. Down below, I'd been awed by the immensity of the mass that was Tintagel. Yet on this ledge hanging over emptiness, air, even below me, the experience of space more vast than the entire headland filled my mind. I felt light and dreamy as if full of reminiscences of bygone eras as I gazed almost mesmerized by the shifting surfaces of waves below reflecting the watery sunlight through parted mist to my eyes.

There was all the space in the world for my mind to wander in, unhampered by the weight of rock, the omnipresence of water, or the tyranny of light. That was the second gift of Tintagel to me: a lifting of the mind into a new awareness of space, a defying of gravity, so obvious on the painful ascent and in daily, two-dimensional living.

To have actually dwelt up in the air like that must have been a delight to the senses and have provided a freedom for the mind rarely experienced in the middle ages when Tintagel was occupied. Perhaps that is what creates the magic of the place and allows one to contemplate possibilities where before only impossibilities existed.

The Gloaming

It was the boats that did it for me,
the bay sloops and the dinghies,
Sliding through the waves,
sailors discussing this or that option,
Voices calm across the swells.
Afternoon races over, the crews harbor bound,
Relaxed in their post-game contentment,
Certain to reach the hoist before the gloaming
Retires shackles and cleats, removing them from easy reach,
In the camaraderie of effort made mutual by common goals.

Sailboats offend not. They rend not the ears, insult not the nose.
They bring joy to all the senses:
Grace of line, perfection of poise, sheets of color,
All things counter and spare,
In the vibrant harmony of tackle and trim.

In their sporting mode,
they survived the rude arrival of the industrial age
Riding out the black storms of coal dust and laid-down grime of soot
With scrubbed decks and new paint.
They battened hatches, stretched awnings, and hunkered down.

Now in the post-industrial era, they ride high again,
Spread new high-tech wings,
grow cams and winches never seen before,
Fledgelings on clean new air.

Inland, beyond the city's glare, in the gloaming,
Man's smear has also dropped from our lovely world.
It's nightfall and flights of duck arrows,

Visible only as plunging black silhouettes against the pale blue of sky,
Wing a swift and silent way towards their evening pond.
Crazy broken honks from geese
tell of their owners' belated fall to water.
Stars drop into sight as if from outside our firmament.
Rags of cirrus float past like yesterday's torn sails,
Emptied of rain, gradually losing the little color they possess.
Calm fills my soul; my time of day has come.

Blessed dark covers what I would not see;
stillness muffles what I would not hear.
Humans are hiding in their houses, eating, watching.
Resting after their struggle to eviscerate Nature by day,
Downing the small survivors
of yesterday's sunny hours.

Northwestering Man has been mauling Nature
since the pyramids, nay longer,
Since he followed the retreating ice and herds of deer
As they meandered towards the flickering sheets of color
in the summer night sky.
Always there was more grass, forest, fish,
though summers came and went
Lands lay behind barriers of water, of mountains, of more people,
Till he met Northeastering Man.
They made agreements, broke faith,
murdered each other, spread disease,
Interbred, and they populated and repopulated
until the lion and the lynx,
Moving away from Man, fell off the map.

I was more innocent then,
Busy with the rhythms of my blood,
Yet knew there'd come a night without a dawn
When no amount of prayer
would turn the ebb into a flood.

Beverly Koepplin

Beverly Koepplin

Two Days Without Wind

The First Day

One mid-April day, my sister Karen and I pedaled our bikes to the nearby country school in Corvallis, Montana. We had been cooped up for a week as a cold wind had been blowing through our valley, and it had been too uncomfortable to be outside for any length of time. Nestled as it was between the Bitterroot and the Sapphire mountain ranges, our valley had acted as a tunnel for the ceaseless moaning winds, and we were heartily tired of the relentless moving air that had battered us day and night. So on that first still day, after the wind had died down and not even the new grass stirred and the aspen trees had quit shaking, we were anxious to be outside.

On this Saturday, the schoolyard was empty. There were no cars in the parking lot, and we had the place to ourselves. We parked our bikes and ran to the playground area. Hopscotch and the monkey bars beckoned. We were free to do whatever we wanted, and we could not contain our happy squeals as we ran amok. Two blocks over, the main street was quiet with few people out and about as most of the local people were at the monthly grange meeting. The sunshine seemed even warmer as we ran and hopped and flew along the monkey bars. At some point, I stopped and sat on a bench to tie my shoe and heard an odd sound, a rustling in the distance like something large was sweeping toward us. But I could see nothing. The wind had not returned, and the trees were still and silent. There was not a soul in sight. No one was running any machinery in the grassy meadow beyond the school. I could not account for the rustling noise. I called to my sister, and she ran over to where I was sitting. I asked her to listen, and cocking her head to one side, she did so. It was obvious by now that the noise was rapidly approaching, and we looked at each other, confused and unsure what to do in the face of this invisible and thus seemingly dangerous thing headed our way. The sound was that of a hundred horses moving quickly, leather creaking and harnesses softly jangling. No voices, no other noises, just this silent army on the move. Even as we stood there, paralyzed and staring wide-eyed at each other, the unbidden and unseen noise surrounded us, pushing us together in a breathless hug. In a matter of moments, the noise had rushed past us and faded in the distance until, at last, silence returned. Without a word, we ran to our bikes, jumped on, and pedaled home as fast as we could. As we put our bikes away, we shook our heads at each other, our code for agreeing that we would not be telling anyone about what had just happened, ever.

The Second Day

One hundred years before, on a mid-April day in 1877, the 7th Cavalry of the United States Army resumed its march through the Bitterroot Valley, chasing Chief Joseph and his Nez Perce tribe south to Lola Pass where the soldiers hoped to capture the tribe and force them onto a reservation in Idaho.

The past week had been hard marching as the days had been windy and cold, and the soldiers and horses both were restless and tired of the constant keening of the wind as it chased them down the Valley. That day in mid-April, the wind had finally stopped and the sun had come out. Thin as it was, the sunshine was welcome, as was the stillness. It felt good to the men to move without being buffeted about, to finally gather up the gear that been blown around, to eat a somewhat leisurely breakfast, and to break camp and move on out in the still air. They mounted their horses and headed south toward Lola, at first laughing and calling to each other in the warmth of the new day, and then settling down into a steady pace. They passed St. Mary's Mission in Stevensville without stopping, intent on putting some miles in while the sun still shone, only waving to Father Ravalli as they rode by. On they pushed, pausing only for water from the Bitterroot River in a meadow located near Corvallis, a small settlement south of Stevensville. The few hardy residents watched the troop as the men saddled back up and wished them well. On the 7th Cavalry moved, apace through the Valley, the horses' hooves pounding, the saddle leather creaking, and the harnesses softly jangling.

Note

It is said that on quiet April days in the Bitterroot Valley, when conditions are just right, you can hear the 7th Cavalry passing through on its way to capture Chief Joseph and his Nez Pearce tribe, the ghostly troop never stopping or talking, the only sound that of the pounding hooves and the creaking leather and the jangling harnesses of the horses.

Epilogue

In October 1877, after traveling over 1500 miles in an effort to elude capture, Chief Joseph surrendered to the 7th Cavalry 40 miles south of the Canadian border. His diminished tribe was ill, freezing, and starving. In his famous speech of surrender, he said "I am tired. My heart is sick and sore. From where the sun now stands, I will fight no more forever."

Beverly Koepplin

Shout out to Conor

Youngest of my darlings, tiniest of my stars,
born with the lightest of red hair, but still red like a young flame,
and I should have known then that there is a spark inside you
that never stops flickering, that never stops growing and glowing.

I love to watch you watching the world, so quietly like a fox pup
and then you move and the air parts for you as you go.
And you do whatever you have decided to do, clearing the path ahead,
still quiet, but resolutely gathering your energy, stoking that flame.

And then you explode, tiny sparks flying from you, around you,
And the bat meets the ball with a resounding crack
or you break into song, some old song you shouldn't even know,
and "The Sea of Love" caroms around the room in your young voice.

Your mind is always on a quest, a crusade really, one without limits.
You help your mother bake so you know what warm dough feels like.
You run in the sun around the track to find out if you can catch a dream.
You comfort a quietly-weeping girl because your heart is that good.

Every minute I spend with you is a minute of wonder,
Every hour you surprise me, every day that I live, you fill with delight.
You are a gift of fire that will warm all of my days and nights.
You are a splendid and never-ending gift, and I thank you for you.

Beverly Koepplin

A Short Walk, a Full Moon

The dusk is slowly falling into the dark
after a long, warm and satiated day.
The promise of a jasmine-scented night fills the air,
and our sweet dreams will be even sweeter for it.

Let us wander down the road for a while,
walk the wine away, watch the moon breach in the sky,
follow the furrows of the road or walk on the berms
hold hands and swing our arms, like children at play.

There was today, there will be tomorrow,
but right now in this time and right here in this place,
we are all that we need, we are all that we want,
and, love, the rising moon will surely guide us home.

Dancing the World Away

She dances under the stars.
Like a wild child Gypsy or a wayward wanton,
she dances as though the moon is playing just for her
and all of the galaxy is the orchestra, just for her.

She dances for herself.
Each footfall is one step closer to freedom,
one step further the world moves away,
one more step her heart takes in healing.

She dances in the night winds
where the breezes catch her sheer scarf
and spread it out into wings so she can fly
when others have tried to pin her down with pain.

She dances away from prying eyes.
Too many people, too many sorrows
have kept her company for too long.
She dances away from their always grasping hands.

She dances in purple satin slippers
which shred with each step on the hard and rocky ground
Yet she dances on, dipping and swaying and floating,
slowly dancing the world away, one step at a time

Beverly Koepplin

Calling Me Home

The birds' songs are calling me home.

The paper lantern in the dark sky lights my way.

By my path, the tree leaves rustle in welcome.

My day is done; I can rest again in my safe harbor.

The simple loaf of bread, the slab of yellow cheese,

and the glass of wine are all I need, all I want.

Comfort seeps in under the door, the walls are warm,

and the very air holds a promise of sweet sleep.

I can move slowly here where time fades to nothing.

I listen to music that rolls around and glides over me.

My world becomes small and whole, rich with dreams,

and I have no need to gaze over fences or prowl the night.

The birds' songs have called me home.

The paper lantern in the sky has wandered off,

and the breeze has stilled, gone off to seek its own rest.

My day is done; I can rest again in my safe harbor.

Full Blown

I am full blown, like a rose,
laid wide open to the sun,
past my pristine show stage
and blazing in full fragrance.

If you were to open me now,
petal by velvet petal, limp and exquisitely soft,
you would hear my soft whispers,
you would drown in my moans.

Are you old enough, are you wise enough?
Can you reach past my full bloom
and ravish my scent, my softness?
Do you dare to drown in my glory?

If you give yourself to me,
I will yet make you whole.
I will teach you of the fullness of time,
the glorious ripeness of age.

I am full blown, gorgeous and sated
with the warmth of the bold gold sun.
My soul rises up and goes toward the light,
toward life . . . because I am passion.

Long Summer Day

Long hot day, the night has come.

Burning sun sets, coolness rises.

Arid earth breathes, small creatures stretch.

Heavy air lifts, the moon has come.

Let us dance, the night has come.

Warmed muscles glide, tiny breezes kiss.

Night jasmine unfurls, fireflies flit.

Evening birds sing, the moon has come.

Let us sleep, the night has come.

Passion ebbs, spent limbs untangle.

Minds melt, skin smooths.

Sleep calls, the moon has come.

Beverly Koepplin

My Dad's Dreams

I call my Dad this early winter evening.

It is not yet 6:00 o'clock, but the daylight is gone.

The dark is his evening companion.

I ask what he is doing.

"I was dreaming." – tired, heavy-voiced,

and I know what he dreams.

Ninety years of dreams, beginning long before these last

assisted-living years of chest pains and cloudy eyes.

Dreams, I am sure, of

cold wintertime church pews,

a German God inside and snorting horses outside;

the Cannonball River rolling in the summer

through the seared plains of North Dakota;

A young tall raw-boned woman

striding beside him for fifty-six years;

railroad yards; flaming grapes;

sawdust hanging in the sun;

sweet sleep-heavy children to carry to bed;

drive-in movies; root beer floats;

summer picnic by the mountain lakes of Montana;

card games when laughter boomed around the house;

dancing a light-stepped waltz with his wife;

children growing and bringing other children into his life;

little boys pulling red wagons;

tall young grandsons grasping his arm as they walk together.

Dreams, yes, simple dreams

lining a road well-traveled,

limning a life well-lived.

Dreams to wrap around himself

at the end of the road, at the end of his life.

Sweet dreams, Dad.

Crystal

You are like a crystal

ever spinning in the light,

and with each turn

you show me the sunshine.

I have learned to catch the reflections.

My hands are never empty.

In the prism of time,

I have learned to hold myself.

In the clear glass of life,

I stand tall in the light.

Whatever else this life brings

through the dark side of time,

you will always be there,

glimmering in the sunlight

like diamonds for my soul

and crystal for my heart.

So Far from Montana

In my heart, I drive straight roads
that go on forever through sweet spring air
and under wide open skies with no frames.
In my life, I drive broken-up streets
that go one block at a time through bloated gray air
and under skies with man-made horizons.

In my life, I work hard through days
defined by paper and metal mechanical noise
and metered out by hours I count till end.
In my heart, I sit on a porch and watch
the leaves glow then burst and fall,
and I have no need to count at all.

In my heart, I spend this time of summer
by a cool river that flows under cottonwood trees
and wonder only how a fishing line can arc just so.
In my life, I know that it is summer time.
But that means only that through the long evenings
I will walk this earth here and pretend it is Montana.

How did I get so far from Montana?

Charlotte

Daughter born of my heart, I carry her there always,

deep in my soul where it does not matter that we share no blood.

I loved her father, I loved her grandmother, and I love her.

Our lifelines intertwine whether we come from the same flesh or not.

Girl gone woman now, grown up into her soul and fitting it perfectly.

Brave and true and sure, kind to children, old ladies and animals.

A girl scout in a sassy short skirt, winking over her shoulder.

Take her hand, she will guide you safely to your next adventure.

Princess in her heart, waving her wand, blessing us with her love.

Ask her anything, and she will tell you true.

Cheat her, and she will scorch the earth beneath your feet.

Deny her, and she will go smoothly around you, leaving you a fool.

Motherless daughter, I would take her for my own

But she belongs to the world – or rather the world belongs to her.

I smile as I watch her go through life, one hand held high in princess wave,

And the other reaching out in love for love.

Beverly Koepplin

The Rain Falls Softly

The rain falls softly
through the dusk and into the dark
so that I cannot see it,
only hear it, washing the night.

Will I dream tonight,
gentle, watercolored dreams
that coddle my soul
so I awake smiling into a June morning?

I think not — there is a frisson
of something, fine and strong
as a thread of steel,
running through the rain,
wrapping around and cutting into my soul.

The silk of the midnight rain
wraps a tiger's tooth.
All of the gentle falling down rain
does not hide the sharp thing
that will rend my life and bring death too near
to me this soft summer night.

I Had a Dream

I had a dream
after I met you and before we went out
that you asked me
"What do you want in a man?"
and that I said...
"Someone who is nice and honest and funny
and who dances like the devil and makes love like an angel –
or is it the other way around?"

Well . . .
You were nice, you were funny, and I thought you were honest.

Well...
You made love like an angel (who had once been a devil).

But . . .
We never danced.
I think you probably don't dance anyway –
You wiggle on the ground like a snake.

Still Hippie Chicks

On an early spring evening we four old hippie chicks met
to celebrate supposedly one's good fortune
but secretly to grieve another one's pain.
And so we smiled and laughed as we always have done,
because as we grow closer to closing the circle of life,
we have learned that laughter heals faster than tears
and that it is a remedy of a kind to remember the good times
that have joined us all.

As the late afternoon grew into evening, the air chilled,
and we gathered closer, our four old bodies lending comfort to each other,
our silver-streaked hairs glistening in the warm light of the lamp.
One of us got up to bring the bottle of wine into the room,
another to find the grass and the rolling papers.
Soon that sweet smell filled the room and smoke streaked the air,
and laughter, like a long curling ribbon, wound around us,
joining us yet again.

For a time that evening, all was right in the world that spun around us
while we pushed it to the edges of our collective consciousness.
There is nothing like the strength of four old hippie chicks.
We could have moved huge boulders over rolling land
and through deep forests and across thundering rivers.
And that is exactly what we did until we had formed our world around us,
Joining us as always.

In the Shadows

In the moonlit shadows of my bedroom
my parents dance a perfect waltz,
gliding slowly in and out of the darkness
to the strains of the Tennessee Waltz.

My mother's hair lies loosely waved on her neck,
her eyes shining with a secret she never shared.
In her best dress and wearing the pearls my father gave her,
she sways silently on her feet, a phantom of grace.

My father holds her in his arms, strong and steady,
as though he will never let her go.
The collar of his white shirt lies stiff against his neck,
his reddened rough farmer's skin hidden in its creases.

In the moonlight, they waltz on and on.
Between and through the columns of light and dark,
they float and swing and dip as they circle the room.
They never stop smiling, and they never stop dancing.

When at last the music fades and the final notes hang in the air,
my father dances my mother to the door,
where she turns and smiles at me, her red lips curving in joy
a gift of love through time, and then dances away, is gone.

Going Home

I wonder where my grandmother's heart went
when it went home.
Surely not back to the mother country
where, as an orphaned girl,
she trundled carts of soldiers' bodies through the streets.
Surely not back to the farm in the North Dakota countryside
where she spent her days spinning in the dust,
like a lost whirling dervish, never finding her way,
blown like the thistles across the brown flat lands.
I don't know that this kind, gentle heart
ever found a home.

I wonder where my mother's heart went
When it went home.
Surely not back to that farm where she worked from dawn to dusk
minding her father and her brothers and the livestock, ever toiling,
doing her homework by the light of a kerosene lamp
and hoping that the words she read would somehow carry her away,
a magic carpet ride to a world where there was sometimes surcease.
I suspect her heart went back to Montana
Because she never found a true home in California.

I wonder where my heart will go

when it goes home.

I know it will not be North Dakota for I, too, was lost there.

I know it will not be the San Joaquin Valley,

where I never found my way, either.

Both are flat lands that run to the edges of the earth

and leave me nowhere to hide.

It might be San Francisco

for somewhere in the fog by the sea,

I found myself.

It could be this Sonoma valley

where the mountains stand guard

over the precious vines and me.

But, no, I think my heart will go back to Montana, too,

and my mother and I will sit by the shores of Lake Como

and listen to peace.

David Lewis

The Professor

The *General La Boeuf College of Southern Arts* in Bilious Bayou, Louisiana, was a proud school. Too damn proud to admit the surrender of Gen. R.E. Lee, as well as Gen. Joseph Johnston and the other dregs of the Confederate States Army. The school still refused to bow to the ridiculous Yankee whims of integration and feminine equality. That is why they were not accredited nor recognized as a school.

All of the professors were graduates of this same school since the graduates could not get a job anywhere else and a graduate from anywhere else would not be interested in this school. The most renowned Professor was Pierre Roget, a native of the parish that was home to the college.

The college was all male and with its limited enrollment, only one fraternity existed and one decrepit fraternity house. The Greek name was no longer known to its members. Since the Greek alphabet was found to be forever unlearnable by potential brothers, the fraternity became known by a comic similarity in English as *Eye Felta Thigh*. This was a name the new members were able to remember even after the first semester.

The college was housed in the former plantation home of its progenitor, General La Boeuf, and the *Eye Felta Thigh* fraternity was housed in the slave quarters of the plantation. These buildings had been updated with running water, electricity, a heating system, and one of the rooms had a modern flush toilet. Since there was never a shortage of rooms, some were rented out. Professor Pierre Roget had leased the plumbed room and two adjacent that were his private laboratories.

Professor Roget was a man of many capabilities and some disabilities and he was identified by various character traits. To a psychiatrist he would be called an idiot savant; to the sheriff he was a pervert; to everyone else in the parish, he was COUSIN.

Professor Roget's passion was ATOMIC COMPRESSION. Modern experiments had revealed that the atoms in a molecule of any material consisted of smaller particles that were separated by finite distances all filled with empty space. If these particles could be squished together, each atom would be very, very, very, small. Imagine the city of New Orleans under a bottle cap.

As Professor Roget configured his laboratory rooms for the study of compression theory, he realized he would need a large amount of energy so he put jumper cables on the 220 Volt clothes dryer. That was his first mistake; his second was expecting that an OUT OF SERVICE sign on the dryer would have meaning to any of the fraternity members.

Heroic Professor Roget decided to use himself as a test item. Obviously this was a case of the ego overtaking good sense since he hadn't developed ATOMIC RE-EXPANSION.

Professor Roget had arranged himself on his pallet, had a drink of de-gasifying fluid and started hooking up the electrodes. At the same time, in the washroom, Petit Lafayette had finished scrubbing his socks, drawers and tee-shirt for Christmas break and tossed them in the dryer. He dialed it over to HIGH HEAT and hit the switch. The lights went out.

In a few days, Professor Roget was considered missing. Investigation of his room revealed a still warm object on his pallet that was not unlike an owl pellet. When the sheriff investigated he found Professor Roget's note explaining the test he had undertaken. Since the pellet on the pallet weighed 280 pounds despite its small size, the coroner declared it was the compressed Professor Roget.

Whatever happened to the partially atomically compressed Professor Roget? He is on display in the anteroom of the *General La Boeuf College of Southern Arts* mounted on a beam-balance scale. Professor Roget's compacted, still warm, pellet balances out against General La Boeuf's Civil War artifacts: a saddle, a dress uniform, an Enfield musket, a canteen full of moonshine, a ceremonial sword and scabbard, a LeMat revolver and for the final balancing, a cask of brandy, forty-two 69 caliber Minié balls, and five cannonballs from a 4-inch Napoleon.

Devil Dan

Little Dan was a likely lad
Robust muscles like his Dad
Ice blue eyes like none other
Curly hair like his mother
Perfect behavior till one day
The ranch remuda got in the way.

Little Dan was mighty sick
His head was pounded by a kick.
When he recovered he had changed
An evil temper and quite deranged.
By the age of twenty there were a lot
That he had fought and he had shot.
Then one day in a fit of rage
He killed every man on the Piscadero Stage.

The Sheriff had a posse sworn
The county's first since Dan was born.
The posse followed the trail he'd ridden
And found the cave where he was hidden.
His gun soon empty, Dan did shout
"Who's man enough to bring me out?"
Dan's father answered - the only one
"I'll bring you out or there will be none."
With bare fists only he crawled on in
The cave roared out a mighty din
In an hour, they both came out
Dan unconscious, the father - near 'bout.

Dan was trussed up on a horse
He finally woke with no remorse.
He cursed and swore and yelled and spit
They put a sack on his head to make him quit.
The Sheriff said, "Son, now hear me talkin
On the gates of Hell you'll soon be knockin
As soon as we get you neck-tied up
We'll have some whiskey in this cup.
Then we'll go to the nearest ranch
And throw the rope over a stout oak branch.
We'll run-off your horse but you will stay
At the end of the rope to swing and sway.
We'll leave you there for the buzzards to share
And no one near 'bouts is going to care."

But the father did care and with not a hope
He jumped on the horse and cut the rope.
And galloped due west for the oceanside
At the shore's highest cliffs he halted the ride,
Cut loose his son and hoisted him high.
Sobbing and moaning he drew a loud sigh
And threw his son to the rocks below
Where waves were thrashing like blowing snow.

When he had seen his son was dead
He shot himself right in the head.
Later his wife, overcome with grief,
Widow of a hero, mother of a thief,
Wanted to be at their side,
Followed the sunset into the tide.

A Dialog Among Two Species

Felix was sauntering down Elm Street in his new home territory with never a care in the world. He was packed with confidence and basking in satisfaction. Felix enjoyed new independence and an abundance of good luck.

Felix was born in a big city where amenities were abundant and available – for humans. Not so good for cats though! Especially not too good for a litter of cats. A mother cat with a litter had a tough time obtaining enough nourishment for herself let alone enough for a kitten cat-feteria. The risks were great too from traffic, stray dogs, the animal control goons, and a lack of food. In addition, she had to frequently move her litter to protect them from marauding Toms that wanted to murder her litter to trigger her breeding instinct anew.

Felix and his littermates were "rescued" by someone who considered themselves a cat saint and turned them over to a temporary home where they were fed by a bottle, their mother never seen again. When weaned, de-wormed and given some shots, they were adopted by someone that felt the need of a companion. Naturally the cutest were the first to find homes and Felix wasn't the first. If records had been kept he may have been tabbed as the smartest of the litter, but now it is just a guess. Felix figured that the smartest thing he had done was skipping his bondage and missing a "fixing" session at the vet. Felix had changed titles from "alley cat" to "rescue cat" to "domestic cat" to his present position of "suburban feral cat." So far, he had enjoyed his new position.

Felix's sashay down Elm Street was always enjoyable. Plenty of shade trees, large houses with big lawns provided a park-like expanse with the necessities of cat life: succulent mice, tender sparrows, and frequent sandboxes and flower beds. Numerous fountains, birdbaths and pools were handy to wet his whistle. He was determined to keep the best stretch of Elm Street as his domain, protected from other male cats.

On a late spring day when fledgling sparrows and plump young mice were easily available, Felix was shocked to hear a piercing whistle, followed by an uncultured voice that shouted, "Whoa, cat! Whatcha doing around here? Skat back to your burrow and don't stop at the sandbox!"

Felix could figure out which house was the source of the voice but his eyesight didn't define the speaker at a distance, so he went closer to the house where the challenger was still following up with more loud whistles. When Felix was closer he saw the ruckus was coming from an open bay window where a large red macaw was dancing on a perch, whistling away – sometimes whole melodies.

Felix ignored the fact that the parrot was about three cat-lengths long from beak to tip of the tail, but he was a little intimidated when the parrot cracked a segment of a Brazil nut in its beak. Felix correctly reasoned that beak could amputate all kinds of cat parts and the macaw's big bright feathers would be a fair defense against cat claws. Yet his ego was bruised by the bossy bird and he answered through the medium of mute-animal telepathy, "Look, you are some damn alien that doesn't even belong in these parts. You aren't natural here. Don't you try to tell us original citizens what to do and what not to do!"

"Listen up, cat. I am not here by choice. Some scum robbed me from a nest with all the other hatchlings to sell us into slavery at pet stores in this country. And how do you figure that this is your country? The Americas didn't have any domestic cats of their own until the damn Europeans brought them over to try to control the vermin and rodents they also brought over. Don't figure you are something intended. Tell that to the ghosts of all the other critters that have become extinct while there are millions of damn cats running loose killing little birds."

Felix hadn't really been aware of cat history in the New World. He didn't know that little tame cats were so popular as human's pets that their numbers were explosive while the same humans murdered the beautiful, big native cats close to extinction. He felt sorry for the beautiful big bird, isolated from any of his kind for the rest of his lifetime just to entertain humans if their television sets were shut off.

"Well, bird, I apologize for my ignorance and I see what a raw deal you got. I'll try to respect your terrain. Maybe we can work together some if you are able to fly around sometime. My name is Felix, by the way, even though the humans called me *Tigger*."

"I agree, Felix, we have to work together even if we don't agree on all things. **Some** sentient creatures have to do what they can to save the Earth. Oh yes, the damn fool humans call me *Polly* but my real name is Jorge."

A Transition

During his breakfast, Professor Philo Lexicon thought of the changes in his life during the past six months as he soaked up a cup of coffee and scanned *The New York Times.* His wife, nicknamed Mona, reflected over the fact that he literally soaked up a cup of coffee every morning. The problem was, Philo had let his facial and cranial hair grow unchecked. Only his **brilliant** green eyes shone out of a thatch of beard, mustache, bangs and braids. His mouth, most of his ears, and nose were pretty well shrouded in his hair. Coffee, in a cup without a straw, was diverted from its course down the gullet by the hair and whiskers that filled the cup, absorbing at least half of the contents. Mona shuddered when she looked too long because he reminded her of a childhood trauma.

When Mona was five years old, her darling Siamese cat had pulled a wren's nest out of a basket on the back porch. The extracted nest had been built neatly and securely in the basket by the wren parents until the darling Siamese cat pulled it out to partially devour the hatchlings. The "partial" part was especially disgusting, and the grieving, twittering, cheeping parents played a dirge for days. Now, Philo, her husband, had a face that looked like that wren's nest with a display of a mass of disheveled hair that looked like grass and twigs. A flood of unpleasant memories followed when she looked at him, which often ended in a migraine headache.

She was now seldom called by her nickname, and she and her

friends had reverted to her maiden name of *Svetlana Pushpin*. The nickname had been tagged on her during the semester after her marriage to Philo. The honeymooners made passionate love for hours at a time and it was signaled to all of the neighbors on the block by Svetlana's long, protracted moans. Her moans had the vocal range of the late Yma Sumac and the persistence of Maria Callas. Even before she had come out to the sunlight, everyone called her "the moaner." When she became social, it was natural to call her Mona.

Since Philo had grown all of that hair, Svetlana wasn't moaning anymore. She was also cross and defensive. More often than not she associated Philo with the wren-nest disaster and not wedded bliss.

Philo's adoption of the hirsute lifestyle had started at a routine dentist visit but he was not really aware of the circumstances. When he went to the dentist, he had a naked face but he had started to change immediately afterward. He had been asleep under a charge of nitrous oxide, or laughing gas. He was only getting a cleaning but he was such a fidgeter that both Philo and the dentist opted for the gas. Philo liked music to attract sleep so he carried an iPod on most occasions. He usually forgot to keep it charged so he handed his charging apparatus to the dentist to plug in after the gas was flowing. The dentist knew nothing about iPods but he saw the charging cable had a connector much like one on the side of his X-ray machine. When he plugged it in, it encountered 15,000 volts, which was more than Philo's iPod was used to. An electric arc emitted that shot between the two earplug speakers. Philo's head was in between the earphones. Smoke curled out of Philo's ears long after the earplugs were removed. The dentist directed his water spray device, intended for spraying freezing water on a tooth's bare nerves, directly into Philo's ears until the smoke stopped. The dentist kept the gas flowing until he had finished a rather cursory cleaning, then he prepared Philo to wake up. He was a little nervous about lingering side effects but when Philo woke–apparently normally–he made no mention of it. The only distress Philo noticed was to the iPod, which just pulsed between an incandescent brilliance to a stodgy gray.

In addition to all of the hair growth, Philo's thinking patterns changed. He was a PhD in linguistics but now his only interest was in a science he was developing called **Lexicon Statistics**. It was based upon measurements which showed that at unexplained intervals, the frequency of use of a word could change from a random distribution to abnormal frequencies of frequent use or, in some instances, an extreme lack of use. No one else was interested in his science project! His teaching ability in other subjects was being neglected, putting his career in jeopardy.

When Philo left for his second dental cleaning appointment six months later, Svetlana begged off the goodbye kiss, claiming a possibly infectious cold. She was actually turned off by his pucker which was surrounded with a portion of a poached egg in his beard and mustache and the remaining coffee, still dripping from his hairy chops.

The dentist was a little surprised at Philo's appearance. He reasoned that the previous gasified shock had caused the problem, so a reversal from Philo's obviously ghastly configuration was more important than the tooth cleaning. After Philo was in a deep, unconscious, gas-induced state, the dentist took the iPod's earplugs out of Philo's ears and slipped one down each pant leg. When the X-ray's 15,000 volts were applied, there was no arc between the ear plugs because of the longer transmission path and various insulators. Despite the lack of the arc, Philo seemed to conduct electricity well and he drew a high current from pant leg to pant leg–the exact path unknown to future scientific study.

When Philo woke up, his eyes were not the **brilliant** green for which he was known. Now they just reflected light and did not emit light. His hair was limp and his face no longer resembled a wren's nest but was more like a freshly shampooed yak. On the way home, Philo had an urge to be shorn and he had a barber remove all facial hair and return to a normal hairstyle. Since his abundant hair had shaded his whole face except for the tips of his ears, everything about his face was untanned and very white, except the ears' tips were a dark tan. This had an unexpected benefit because now Philo reminded Mona of her darling Siamese cat instead of the unkempt wren's nest.

Did you notice that she is called Mona again rather than Svetlana?

This was all because Philo and Mona had returned to their previous post-nuptial state of happiness. Not only was Philo's appearance corrected by the experiment of the dentist, Dr. Frankenstein, but Philo's attitude and intellect rebooted to a productive state.

Dr. Frankenstein dropped all of his clients and rode his moment of accidental fame to a stressless job as a Fox TV News commentator, making verbose comments on topics of which he knew nothing.

Mugsy and the Parrot

Mugsy had been out of jail for just a month following an eight-year sentence for felony robbery. Any good intentions had disappeared as fast as his meager stash of cash and he was now, this very minute, starting a brand new criminal pursuit. He was going to break into the mansion of one of those Silicon Valley billionaires. He figured a bundle of money and valuables must be available. Hell, there was probably a hundred grand in the sofa cushions. He wasn't worried about the owner, who was in Russia prepping for a one-month trip to the space station. Mugsy was sure security would be slackened with the owner gone, dogs in the kennel, the help on a holiday and only the automatic systems in place. Mugsy knew the automatic systems well and had even worked for an outfit for a month to learn the ropes. Mugsy forgot that his information was over eight years old.

Mugsy had cased the mansion day and night for weeks. It had taken a while to find a weak spot. The five acres of grounds were surrounded by a 12-foot-high bronze fence with spikes at the top, and an electrometer told him it had several thousand volts of rapidly pulsating "juice". A beautiful old Canary Island date palm had been permitted to live, in spite of its proximity to the fence. It was a monkey highway over the fence and Mugsy was a pretty good climber himself. He would just have to rappel down about 30 feet where it leaned over the fence.

Mugsy had night-vision goggles and an infra-red torch so he

wouldn't give himself away with a moving light like he did on a previous break-in when he got busted ten years ago. He had waited for the most meager moon, discombobulated the alarm system, cut out a pane of glass, and picked a lock. He was in the house within 15 minutes and he wandered around getting used to the gray-green world of night-vision goggles. He had surgical gloves and a face mask which he put on as soon as he was over the fence. He looked for the "Man Cave" where he figured the pickings would be best. He had seen, but wasn't allowed to copy, the architect's floor plan at the city planning office. He soon was in the man cave, four thousand square feet and a 20-foot ceiling. It was a museum, office, and taxidermy zoo. A lot of obviously expensive stuff but most was too heavy to carry back up the rope to the date palm. He wanted gold, diamonds and money.

After about five minutes of wandering around sizing up loot against his backpack, Mugsy was startled by a harsh voice.

"AWK. Well hello, Mugsy. You must be missing the San Quentin chow. Here you are and you will be back in stir before the fuzz gets your old paperwork filed in the DISMISSED - TIME SERVED archive!"

"Who the hell is calling my name and where are you? You are a soon-to-be-dead SOB, I'm telling you now," screamed Mugsy.

"I'm the boss's parrot. Name is Ichabod Quantico but everyone calls me IQ. That is because I am as smart as hell, like all of my kind, and my I.Q. is over 150 and I know yours is 87. For instance I know that you took the name Mugsy at the Crescent City jail when you were 19 because you were getting too much grief from your real name of **Preston Folded**. That was a too damn funny name thought of by your old man, **Hans Folded**, the last time your mother saw him. Took it off a laundry ticket, the most reading he had done since his 3 years at school. Your mother, **Chastity Folded**, knew a lot of men that thought you had a damn funny name too, and they told you so, usually 5 or 10 a night.

I have a TV picture of you climbing up the palm tree. Sent your picture, weight, and height data to the FBI and I had your full dossier in 38 seconds. A SWAT team is on the way over here. They know that you have a Colt .45 automatic from the magnetometer and scanning X-ray in that tree. They have a damn good excuse to take you out without any dialog as long as you are carrying that gun. I call that palm tree *The Yellow Brick Road* because so many damn fools come down it. You took the bait just like the other dumb punks that have tried," said IQ the parrot.

Mugsy was livid! "Damn bird!" he yelled, "I'll wring your neck till it looks like a candy licorice stick."

"TRY IT!" said IQ. "There is a TASER on my perch with 5 voltage levels. Number 1 will have you dancing. Number 2 will have you on the floor. Number 3 will have your balls smoking. You won't need any more unless you are a charging bull elephant. Follow my directions or that stuffed owl to the right of you will zap you with enough focused ultrasound energy to make your eardrums explode like overripe eggs. Notice that his head is turning to watch you just like the real thing."

"Now!" said the parrot. "Throw the gun on the floor, lest perchance, you decide to shoot yourself. Turn on the lights and find 3 pair of handcuffs hanging on the coatrack. Put one pair on your ankles, snap a cuff from the second over the chain on the ankles and the second cuff on the chain of the third. Put one cuff of the third on your left hand and pass the other through your crotch with your right hand. Then close the last one on your right wrist by pushing against the wall. Lie on the floor while I ring the cops in."

The police did come in and bundle Mugsy, meek and confused, into a squad car. A sergeant came back, picked up a flash drive and a printout coming out of the printer. He had TV pictures, audio, and the FBI files on Mugsy's latest caper. "Damn" he said, "this is the tenth crook that parrot robot has nailed this year."

David Lewis

Caesar's Revenge

"Mr. Jones," I said as I polished a prime apple, a 99¢ Delicious, and placed it on his desk, "you gave me a failing mark on my translation of Caesar just because I missed three words." Mr. Jones was my Latin teacher and he seemed to regret that the Empire had tumbled in 400 something AD. He would go back in a minute if he could and he'd wear one of those toga things and drive a chariot too. Until Mr. Jones got hold of us, the only time I'd seen a toga was on John Belushi when he wore one in the *Animal House* movie. Mr. Jones wore one to read us a speech from some dead Roman. It might have impressed the class if we really knew any Latin because Mr. Jones didn't do it in English.

We figured that Mr. Jones wore it to impress Ms. Ford, the cute Home Economics teacher. Ms. Ford is no relation to *The Ford* associated with automobiles but she did have a distinctive chassis and bumpers. Why Mr. Jones thought that showing off his legs – they could be mistaken for a German shepherd's–and yes, I mean the dog, not an actual German with a flock of sheep–would wow Ms. Ford was beyond all of his pupils. That was obviously the cause, however, because Mr. Jones blushed and stammered whenever Ms. Ford showed up. Mr. Jones knew more Latin than a lot of old Romans and he would converse in Latin in class just to impress us. Naturally the pupils caught on to only a smidgen. But there is nothing funnier than a grown man stammering in Latin. That in turn made Ms. Ford giggle, which thrilled all of the boys in class because it caused a lot of oscillation around her diaphragm. Mr. Jones, however, got a glazed look in his eyes like a warrior who sat on a catapult just after the launch, and stammered all the more. "ET...et...et," he repeated with a rapidity that sounded like a Roman jackhammer, until his breath gave out and he turned red.

"My goodness Cyrus," said Ms. Ford. "Do relax and lend me your stapler."

That is when we learned Mr. Jones' name. He always went by C.D. Jones in the annuals and all the students were to address him as Mr. Jones. Mr. Jones was not proud of his name. When Ms. Ford spoke it, it had a nice ring to it and sounded distinguished. This made Mr. Jones blush a deeper crimson than the oxygen-deprivation crimson.

Mr. Jones fiddled in the desk drawers for the stapler, then fiddled in his drawers to smooth the toga, and then tried his best not to look embarrassed. Ms. Ford sashayed out of our class and Mr. Jones began to breathe, loaded us up with homework, and excused the class.

As I was telling Mr. Jones earlier, he had given me a failing grade for a small mistake on a test and it could impact my passing the Latin class – which I didn't want to repeat in the summer.

Mr. Jones said, "ET TU BRUTE does not translate to 'I had two burgers.' If you want to be a wise-ass and insult the great Caesar, you can try it in the summer instead of driving your convertible up and down Hempsted Avenue through July and August and leaving long, ugly tire tracks." He was about to get into rage mode but he started to blush and stammer. Behind me, Ms. Ford had come on the scene.

"What is the talk about convertibles, Cyrus? I just love convertibles. They make me—so carefree," cooed Ms. Ford.

"Well," I popped in, "I was just asking Mr. Jones if he would like to try out my convertible during the weekend. The dealer doesn't have the deluxe model of the Pantera Lioness in stock and Mr. Jones was interested in buying one but wisely wanted to try one first. They must be driven carefully or the acceleration can make the wheels spin and can absolutely pin the passenger into the seat. Since they have to be ordered from a custom shop in Italy it would be a while before one will be stateside, and naturally they get gobbled up before many get to drive one. There is probably a waiting list also to consider. I'm sure Mr. Jones would give you a spin if he cares to try mine out."

Mr. Jones turned white, red, white in a long succession. He seemed to be doing rapid calculations in his head while looking at Ms. Ford with a glassy-eyed stare.

Mr. Jones said, "Yes, very well, Marcus, if you would drop off the keys and the manual Friday afternoon, you can tell me a few of its foibles. In the meantime, you can think of how you will enjoy your place on the **Latin Honor Roll**. Yes, very well, you may go now."

"*Veni vidi vici*," I said as I left. The last Latin I have uttered.

Frog Seeks Princess

Frog seeks a princess, not to be changed but to be kissed; a kiss with **a taste electric.**

Frog does not want the princess's castle or the vault, the crown or the scepter, these are for the royal heirs. Frog seeks only a kiss with **a taste electric.**

For the proper princess, Frog wants to share: the hoot of the owl, the croak of the raven, the caw of the crow, the whistle of the hawk, the coo of the dove, the crow of the rooster, the trill of the thrush, the hail of a quail and a kiss with **a taste electric.**

Frog wants to share: the fragrance of the firs, the majesty of the redwoods, the blush of the rose, the waves in tall grass, the palette of the spring flowers, the scent of lilac and a kiss with **a taste electric.**

Frog wants to share: the clarity of prose, the subtlety of poetry, the thought of the essay, the imagination of the novel, the humor of the bon mot and a kiss with **a taste electric.**

Frog wants to share: the baying of the hound, the bark of the seal, the meow of the cat, the nicker of the horse, the lowing of the cow, the bugle of the elk, the song of the whale, the chirp of a mother mouse, the motions of a mime and a kiss with **a taste electric.**

Frog wants to share: the cadence of the surf, the commotion of the ocean, the soliloquy of a brook that does not babble, the cascade of a stream that changes elevation with great elation, the accented language of a wave of distant origin and a kiss with **a taste electric.**

Frog wants to share: the fox's den, the oriole's nest, the lion's lair, the puffin's crag, the pack rat's wealth, a hunter's stealth and a kiss with **a taste electric.**

Frog wants to share things seldom seen: the hyena's frown, an obese clown, a capitalized improper noun, a golfing green turned brown, a ghost town's downtown, a small town's uptown and a kiss with **a taste electric.**

Frog wants to share: the romance of a dance, the fun of a pun, the choice of a chance, the glee of "whee," the joy of a toy, a ploy by the coy and a kiss with **a taste electric.**

Frog wants to share: the breath of love, the whisper of a secret, the hint of infatuation, the shadow of a doubt, the butterfly in the stomach and a kiss with **a taste electric.**

Frog wants to share: a picnic by the bay, a picnic by the harbor, a picnic by the beach, a picnic in a dale, a picnic by a tarn and a kiss with **a taste electric.**

Frog wants to share: a stroll on the beach, a sashay through town, a walk in the park, a saunter through the gallery, an amble on a country road and a kiss with **a taste electric.**

Frog wants to share: the sunset by the ocean, the moonrise over the fields, the moonrise at sunset, the twinkle of the stars, the hastening meteor, the atoms of the universe and a kiss with **a taste electric.**

Frog wants to share: a caress by a fire, a healing touch, a tender massage, a stroke through the hair, a nibble at the nape of the neck and a kiss with **a taste electric**.

Frog wishes to extol: the honor of truth, the infallibility of faithfulness, the equality of the sexes, the respect shown by chivalry and a kiss with **a taste electric**.

Frog scorns: the greenness of envy, the weight of a lie, the corrosion of jealousy, the blight of bigotry and the need for greed.

In the odd moment when other distractions are muted and reflection would be in order, the principal thought should be - a kiss with **a taste electric.**

EPILOGUE

The princess met Frog and thought him very green. After she had shared Frog's delights and tasted a succession of electric kisses she saw that her perception of Frog's green was fading.

Frog loved the princess and loudly called her name, "Briget, Briget, Briget!"

Robyn Makaruk

Stairway to the Stars

Ribbons of fog painted the rails with a lip gloss shine
that beat out the brilliance of the full moon.
The cable car announced its arrival at the bottom of the hill
with squeals of iron-on-iron,
and the ratchet of the pulling on brakes.

In the damp night air,
the grip man rapped out his signature tattoo on the bell.
It was the last run of the night
to pick up the handful of bloodshot eyes
from the *Buena Vista*.

The bartender had listened to the same old stories about
the glory days of conquests and failures.
He responded to calls of "play it again, Sam" as they
nursed glasses of broken dreams
all the while dressing their damaged hearts in camouflage.

"Last call, ladies and gentlemen,"
and when the trysting hour approached
he purposely mixed the last
'one for the road' on the light side.
A repeat of the tattoo from the cable car's bell
drove all who might ride across the street.

A deep baritone voice rang out
"All Aboard on your Stairway to the Stars.
Hang on tight, it's a mighty climb,"
his voice merging with the melancholy sound
of the fog horns echoing across the Bay.

The Haunted Birdhouse

On a visit to a country store that advertised 'real & genuine antique artifacts', I came upon an unusual birdhouse. It was made from a variety of wood scraps, none very identifiable, but it had a certain character. Shaped like a two story miniature Victorian with dainty gingerbread trim, it looked more like a doll's house. The name "Stroud" and a date of 1923 were carved on the bottom. I'd been looking for another birdhouse to accompany my chickadee nesting box, and hoped to attract the nearby bluebirds that were coming into nesting season. The box could be ideally located in my back yard, close to the open fields but sheltered and protected from predators, so I made the purchase.

I hung it on a tree about 10 feet from the chickadee box on a windy morning, and this strange sound started coming from it. The sides of the house had a few cracks in the wood, and the nest hole seemed normal, but the direction of the wind focused on this new birdhouse almost like a mini tornado. There was this agonizing groaning coming from it. The chickadee box did not move an inch, nor was it affected by the wind. I didn't think much about this and waited until the wind died down in the evening when everything seemed to return to normal.

The next day I checked on the two houses, and things seemed to be normal. The house finches, goldfinches, towhees, sparrows, titmice, scrub jays and hummingbirds came to the nearby feeders and flew over to the wall fountain for water. Nothing seemed out of the ordinary until late in the afternoon when a wind came up, and again these gruesome sounds started coming from the newly purchased birdhouse. The wind directed its force only to the new birdhouse, not the chickadee box, nor any of the feeders. Even the wind chimes did not ring. This new box swung, swayed, moaned and groaned. I took it down from its place and set it on the ground.

Next morning I checked the feeders, chickadee box and new house that had been set on the ground. All was calm, until once again, later in the day, a wind came up and directed itself right at the new birdhouse on the ground. The same sounds emanated from it and the wind force blew it over to expose the name and date on the bottom. Then the noises changed to gentle, whining and whimpering sounds.

When I explained all of this activity to my partner, he dowsed it. His arm holding the dowsing rod started to shake and the rod swung violently in a crosswise movement indicating this birdhouse had very bad energy or 'mojo'. This was repeated at another time during the day with the same conclusion. His recommendation was that no amount of 'cleansing' would heal the bad energy in this birdhouse and it should be destroyed.

On researching the origin of the name Stroud, it appeared that my birdhouse could have been made by Robert Stroud, known as Birdman of Leavenworth, and also known as The Birdman of Alcatraz. It was during his incarceration at Leavenworth, Kansas, that he did indeed raise birds (mainly canaries) and became a noted ornithologist. However, this man was a psychopath, a very dangerous criminal who was incarcerated from 1909 until 1959, and then sent to a medical center for federal prisoners in Springfield, Missouri, until he died in 1963. My birdhouse was most likely made by Robert Stroud when he was in Leavenworth, and there was no way that I would be raising dear little bluebird families in this house haunted by the ghost of Robert Stroud.

I burned the birdhouse in a fire pit, and in the process that strange wind returned, fanning the flames in the pit, issuing gentle sighing sounds that sounded like a release. In a short time all there was left was a small pile of purple ashes that I scooped into a paper bag. On the next stormy day, I drove to the coast and cast the bag into Pacific Ocean on the outgoing tide.

Mirror Image

His anxiety level was at boiling point as he raced across town to catch the last ferry. It had been a rotten day dealing with some of the company's most important clients trying to negotiate their way to a more acceptable resolution to their dastardly deeds. Well, that's what high-paid defense lawyers did, and his head was pounding thinking about how the team had to defend their clients and offer some mitigations without stepping outside the law.

The last of the passengers were making their way up the boarding ramp, and he just had time to text in his drink order to the bar before the announcement came for 'all aboard' as he joined the last handful of commuters. The bartender had his double martini ready and he made his way down to the lower level where the techies seated at small tables were already working on their various devices, smartphones, tablets, laptops and the like. He found a table, opened his laptop and pulled up the brief he was working on. This job was killing him, as his physician had reminded him every time he saw him. "You've got to find some way to reduce your stress levels, Aaron. Look at these lab results. You're off the charts in all the critical areas."

The ferry horn rang out and the 'all aboard' message came over the address system as a final call. Aaron looked up as the boarding ramp was beginning to retract and saw an unshaven man, limping with what looked like a prosthetic limb coming towards the ramp. He had long, dark hair, a full beard, a large backpack, and was carrying what looked like an instrument case. The employee lowered the ramp again and went to assist the last passenger, then the ferry closed the doors and started moving on out. Shortly the limping man made his way down to the lower deck and eased into a corner across from Aaron, taking time to move the stiff left leg into place before he settled into the chair. Aaron was surprised at how the man looked and caught the man's mirror image in the ferry's corner window. His face looked fierce, dark and foreboding, almost evil. Sunken cheeks, steel-blue eyes, and long hair tied back with a clip of sorts. He was too polite to stare, but in his profession he'd developed a sure sense of a person's character from what was offered in a first impression, and this one boded ill. The stranger sat with closed eyes for some time while the ferry plowed across the Bay. He seemed to go deep within himself. Aaron texted the bar for a second martini and got up to climb the stairs to the upper deck. On returning he saw the stranger undo the hair clip, bend down, open the instrument case and take out a classical guitar then clamp his hair clip on the upper frets. He ran beautifully manicured hands over the instrument and softly touched each string for tuning. He lifted the guitar and started to play one of the most romantic guitar pieces known, *Romance d'Amour*. Every head in the room lifted from devices and turned toward the stranger. The low sound of the ferry engines did not deter from the beauty of the music. Time seemed to stop. Aaron's realization of his judgment of the stranger came to smack him right in the gut. How unimportant his job of stress and anxiety seemed when he could be transformed by beautiful sounds. When the last note was played, he got up and walked to the stranger and introduced himself. "My name is Aaron Metzner, and I am an asshole lawyer. The gift of your music today has awoken in me a renewed promise to myself that I will open my heart and listen to the world before seeing it with judgmental eyes and mind." The stranger nodded as if he knew what he was doing before putting his guitar in the case.

Olé

He sat in a corner of the crowded room,
a glass of *tinto* within reach
waiting for the dancer's entrance.

The guitars began the introduction to *soleares,*
joined by the *palmero* adding *palmas* to the
unique twelve-beat phrases.

The haunting familiarity brought back memories
of his victories in the bullring and the
parties afterwards, guitars, singers and dancers,
the *duende* lasting until sunrise.

It seemed like yesterday when
on that fateful Sunday in Spain's oldest bullring
he led the procession,
the band playing the bullfighter's song,
La Virgen de la Macarena.

And after he made the traditional bow
to the dignitaries and to the crowd
was announced as *El Matador de las Veces,*
'Matador of the Times'.

The bull that day was a large, roaring, cannon of strength.
The fight was long,
and when it came time for the final short sword thrust
he relived the moment as it found its mark
giving the Brave One a swift death.

In its final gesture
the bull fell towards him,
one of its horns ripping into his upper body.

The rustle of a gown sweeping across the stage
brought him back to the present.
Slowly, the music followed the dancer's movements,
her heels responding first with a tremor,
a quiver, building to vibrations
that entered his body waking latent passion.

Then in a transfer of energy, of power,
he sensed her touch, one of healing.
He felt her reaching out to him, sharing his suffering,
soothing his pain.

And in that crowded room
his tears rendered him whole, once more.

The Last Kiss

Tendrils of fog rose from the river and drifted across the bridge. Tatiana had agreed to the tryst but only if they could meet at night and walk to the small hotel on the outskirts of the city for their clandestine rendezvous.

She had given a lot of thought to her dress choice as she laced up a sheer black bustier and black-and-red garter belt. Her black silk stockings were such an extravagance, but she knew that this night of passion would be like no other and had made the decision to purchase them on the black market at no small risk. Her toilette had taken an hour or more, as she languished in the bathtub until the water went cold, then the other extravagance, a small puff of "Evening in Paris" from her crystal atomizer.

She took great care in applying makeup, mascara, powder from an elegant compact, rouge to her cheekbones, and a lipstick that was blotted to retain the dark red color. Some touchup items were added to her handbag as well as a white handkerchief edged with lace. Topping the silk crimson dress was a well-worn, but well-designed overcoat and cashmere scarf. The high heels were not made for walking, but the ensemble did not bear clumsy walking shoes and she knew her feet would be sore from walking on cobblestones even though it was not too long a distance to the hotel.

Leaving her room she inhaled the dampness of the night and started out towards the bridge. The melancholy moan of a foghorn reminded her that this was a coastal city with treacherous waters not too far in the distance. She shivered and thought, "Someone's walking over my grave".

The 'tic, tic' of her heels changed cadence when she stepped on to the metal grating that was the bridge's walkway. A few yards ahead she saw the outline of a figure, a tall person in a long overcoat. As she approached, he turned and said, "Tatiana, you came, Cherie". She smiled and said, "Of course, Yves, you knew I would. I was looking forward to this moment for days." He took her arm saying "Come, let's walk briskly...I would have liked to call a taxi, but you insisted we walk. I have everything arranged at the hotel, including champagne and caviar."

When they arrived the concierge discreetly turned away as the couple took the stairs to the room. Yves opened the door and escorted her into the inviting chamber with, as he said, champagne on ice and caviar waiting in an intimate seating arrangement across from the canopied bed. He took her coat and scarf and ran his hands down her back that suggested they not wait, so she began to slip out of the dress revealing the lingerie that she had so carefully chosen. She had even rouged her nipples that were very evident through the black lace, and Yves was beginning to see that there should be no wasted time.

By the time she had shed her clothes and slipped under the satin sheets, Yves was ready. The lamps were lowered, and they began the age-old ritual of making love. Of course, the French have their own style, especially in the art of kissing, but Tatiana was well versed in the ancient ways of the Kama Sutra. Their lovemaking lasted for hours, until finally she said, "My darling...I must leave now. Please give me my handbag." She pulled out her lipstick as if to apply it, and shot him with a 4.5mm one-shot lipstick pistol, standard KGB issue, known as the *Kiss of Death*.

She rose from the bed, dressed, went to the window, waved her handkerchief four times, and left the hotel. Another tall cloaked figure approached her and said, "Tatiana, you have served Mother Russia well. I have arranged a flight to Moscow in two hours and you will be given a Soviet hero's welcome."

A black sedan pulled to the curb and the two were driven off.

The Attic

The crippled man took a long time to climb three stories to the attic of an ancestral home. Service to his country had left him with a knee-down prosthesis in one leg, a frozen-in-place claw-like hand, and very limited eyesight. It was not that he was an old warrior, his forty-first birthday recently celebrated, but the physical limitations of his war wounds plagued his every motion. His mental acuity was not impaired though; to the contrary, he was in full command of all faculties.

The antebellum home in a Southern state was a sprawling mansion sitting in the middle of what once was seven hundred acres of a rich plantation that had sustained and supported a community of 75 persons, 65 of which were the landowner's slaves. The last remaining member of the Douglas family, Thurmond, had died five years earlier and bequeathed his entire estate to his nephew, Beauregard.

The details of his uncle's will and the terms of Beau's inheritance were outlined and made clear by the attorney who was named as a trustee. Beau was the sole beneficiary of Thurmond's estate with the caveat that he had to read the instructions written in a book labeled with Beau's name that his uncle had stored in a trunk in the attic of the old house. Then he had to sign an affidavit that he understood and would abide by all that his uncle, Thurmond, had set forth in that book. He would then receive the full inheritance, to be administered by the trustee.

The last few steps to the attic were grueling for Beau, and he had to fumble for the key he was given to the door. Cobwebs were swept aside and there was evidence of rodents who were obviously the privileged occupants of the landing area. This place had not been entered for ages, was the first thought that came to Beau's mind as he opened a creaky door, but the dry, dusty odor in the attic boded some goodwill of not being moldy and dank. An ancient steamer trunk stood in the middle of the floor. Beau took a second key and opened it. The contents revealed various bound logs stacked in chronological order, and laid on top was a leather-bound book with Beau's full name on the cover. The light in the attic was fading, so Beau retrieved the book and proceeded to return to a living room in the old house. The descent was painstakingly slow as all his energy had been expended on climbing the stairs.

It was close to midnight before Beau finished reading the contents of the book. There was a numbered summary of the contents at the beginning of the book with full explanation of what those items were and how they came about. His uncle's elegant, handwritten instructions were very clear.

The basic premise of Beau's inheritance was that he was to continue the work that his uncle had given his life to, that of philanthropic causes and playing a role in the families of all who had lived on the estate. Over the decades, the slaves were given their freedom and also ownership of blocks of land that their families had lived on during the Civil War. Thurmond, the last surviving member of the Douglas family, had carried on running the plantation, now just 100 acres, and employing workers to raise organic produce. It was up to Beau to take up the banner and carry on in the family's name.

But the final instruction that Beau read was the one that came as the greatest shock. Thurmond had written that the inheritance of his estate was not just his bequest to Beau, but that the entire estate was Beau's birthright. Thurmond was Beau's biological father, his mother dying in childbirth before they were married. Thurmond's sister and brother-in-law, both now deceased, had agreed to raise Beau as their own, and the true identity of his birth parents would not be revealed to him until Thurmond's death.

Feather of Eagle

He struggled to bring air to his lungs after riding the rapids
that propelled them both over fifty-foot falls.
His grip was still strong
on the child he'd carried through the ordeal
who lay lifeless yet,
but after administering his own healing breath
there came a flutter of eyes,
then coughing, spewing,
and the young one returned to the living.

The Tribe welcomed them both back to the village,
their voices raised
in songs of praise for such bravery.
Before the Tribal Council,
the young warrior recounted how he'd
tracked the child for two days before reaching him
wading into the river.

The Chief spoke: "I give you this Feather of Eagle
through whom the Great Spirit speaks to us about life.
It symbolizes trust, honor, strength, wisdom,
power, freedom and more.
It is sacred to all our People.
Wear it with pride."

Robyn Makaruk

Ode to a Sacred Clown

I saw you, *Heyoka,*
known in our Tribe as the revered one,
presenting yourself in the form of a crow, a survivor,
your resourcefulness, curiosity and adaptability
masked by your mischievous showmanship.

I saw you, *Heyoka,*
when you scaled down the ropes of others' egos
and danced on the Plaza acting the clown,
the crazy one, the trickster.

I saw you, *Heyoka.*
Through your eyes of a child you showed the strangers
in the crowd for what they really were
tyrants, exploiters.

I saw you, *Heyoka.*
You ripped apart prejudices with your strange antics.
When they threw coins at you for your performance
little did they know that you are the king of hoarders
and shining objects.

I saw you, *Heyoka,*
your regal midnight cloak glistening in the firelight.
You were the magnificence of all good things human,
the discounter of all things gone wrong.

I saw you, *Heyoka,*
when you acted the idiot prancing, dancing and feinting,
showing us, those who know,
That you are the Wise One

Charmed

The fragrance of spices wafting across the souk
speak of romance, mystery and stories that tell of danger,
told both in the words of mystics and
in the minds of the tellers.

A traveller enters the scene.
The seductive tones of a flute lure him across the bazaar.
An aged man, seated before a woven basket,
plays a gourd-flute, swaying with the music.

The stranger stands before them transfixed,
and in that moment the music and surroundings
transport him to another place.

A cobra rises slowly from the basket mirroring
the movements of the old man,
hooded eyes focused on some unseen place.

The reptile performs dazzling feats of rising to fill the air
then in blinding changes, softens.
The stranger is at a loss to understand the power
of being woven into that alien strangeness.

A darting movement sends a shaft of impending harm
leaving only a fragmentary glance
at the poison
glistening on the snake.

Robyn Makaruk

Merlin's Apprentice

The young boy climbed the last flight of stairs to the attic in the house where he had lived for the past year. The occupant heard his footsteps and greeted him in a strange language. It had been six years since he was pulled from the wreckage of his parents' burning vehicle after it had been hit head-on by a drunk driver. There was nothing to identify the toddler except for a bracelet on his wrist, engraved with the words *One of the Forest*.

For several years the child lived in an orphanage. The administrator, a kind woman, named him Francis, after the saint, as he was very gentle, had special connections to the birds and animals, and possessed knowledge and wisdom well beyond his years. News of this orphan boy spread. A man whom the locals called "The Hermit" lived several miles away in a remote area close to a forest and, when he learned of the lad's circumstance, came to visit Francis, decided to adopt him and raise him as his own.

Francis was amazed when they arrived at the hermit's home. It was four stories, each with its own separate roofline, like a Scandinavian stave church. The rooms on each story had casement windows that opened to the rolling landscape and forest beyond. A fenced pasture surrounded the house with sheep, goats, llamas and other small animals, grazing together. On entering the house, the hermit said, "Well, Francis, this is your home now. My name is Merlin and I want you to be yourself here. I will show you things you never dreamed of and teach you the art of magic for the human good. You will want for nothing and we shall learn from each other, as we both have been given special gifts."

Merlin had a secret. On his usual walk in the woods six months earlier, he heard a raven calling in a human-like voice, not the normal cronking calls of these birds. He followed the sound and came across a female that had been caught in a poacher's snare. It was unusual that it had been trapped in this way, as ravens are very suspicious and wary creatures, but this snare had been cleverly concealed in the undergrowth and the poacher had dropped a shiny object next to it that drew the raven close. A wire had torqued around her left foot, which on first glance appeared to have severed it.

The raven lay on the ground on her side, with terror in her eyes, but when Merlin approached she breathed, "Help me." Her life force was ebbing, so she must have been there for some time. Merlin carefully released the wire, wrapped the beautiful bird in his cloak and carried her home. On inspection the raven's left foot was still attached so he skillfully removed the foot and placed it in preservatives. He then called upon his powers to heal her. He concocted a brew of herbs and made a poultice to apply to the damaged leg without the foot. All the while he spoke to her in an unusual language that became their communion. He brought her grubs, snails, even eggs from his hens, which she hastily consumed.

Merlin had amazing carpentry skills, and crafted a cradle device in which she could elevate her body and rest in until she gained enough strength to stand on the one good leg. Day by day she improved and they developed a strange dialogue wherein they shared stories of other worlds. Merlin saw that she would live and he took it upon himself to make her fully functional as a raven once more. He named her *Nike*, after the winged goddess of victory.

Merlin had another secret. Not only was he a mystic, but he had working knowledge of a 3-D printer that could be programmed to fabricate three-dimensional objects. There were already successes in the medical field not only with the production of internal organ parts but other objects as well. One story of his house contained a clean room, laboratory, computers and a 3-D printer. He knew it was his destiny to fabricate a new foot for *Nike*, one that would not only be a prosthetic device, but a fully functional raven's foot.

When Francis came to live with them he bonded immediately with *Nike*, and communicated in the same almost-but-not-really language that Merlin and she spoke. Francis had the task of helping *Nike* with the more mundane tasks of personal grooming and she developed soft crooning vocals when he stroked her glossy feathers. Francis knew that Merlin would somehow mend *Nike's* foot, and when he showed him how he would fabricate a new foot for her, he was excited to be part of the plan. The computer model was designed. It had been a challenge to replicate a fully articulated foot that would grow on to a leg, but all was in place and the project was completed in four days. Because of Francis' special connection to *Nike*, he was the one to soothe the raven and gently tell her about how the procedure to connect a new foot would unfold and that when she woke from the anesthetic, she would have a new foot and live up to her name.

Nike was waiting in her top-floor attic room when Francis climbed the stairs that day. When he opened the door, she said, "I was the one who told Merlin of your plight and that he should bring you here. You and Merlin have given me my life, just as Merlin has given you yours. We three will be connected forever." She hopped off her cradle on two legs, waddled over to Francis, spread magnificent wings, and flew out the open window.

Birds of Passage

When I look up to the skies
And see those who fly with nary a care
Soaring in a freedom we mortals only dream of
An image comes to mind's eye
Of an encounter with a Raven
Creature of myth and mystery
Descendant of dinosaurs

I see Raven as one of my ancestors
We are just energy, after all
Birds of passage, so to speak
Touching down for a time

We think we're putting down roots
But in the small window of a lifespan
They are shallow anchors
And don't count for more than a hill of beans
Upon which we alight for a speck of time

I know that while I exist
I am but a drop
In this vast ocean of livingness
And when I leave
I will join all the Birds of Passage
And return to **Stardust**

Robyn Makaruk

Nocturne

I see you, Queen of the Night,
dismissing the rosy clouds
while you usher in the crescent moon
and gather the stars,
your arms open in invitation
for me to join you in your nocturnal delights.

I wonder where you'll take me tonight?
Will you send me to a distant planet
to dance above the clouds in an iridescent gown
with a band of noisy stars?

I'm still here on the Blue Planet,
but know my time is measured.
Who knows how long it will be
before I can join you?
But I do know from where I've come
and to where I'll go,
for I, like you,
am **Stardust**.

Phoenix

Last night
as I traveled through the mist
I met you
a glorious, beautiful, red bird of fire.
You had built yourself a pyre
and set yourself ablaze,
an act of sacrificing self for renewal.

I saw you rise, reborn, and
with your new strength
fly to the heights of the sky
to lay your ashes
at the altar of the Sun.

You and I are children of the Sun
and we will live eternally through
birth, death and renewal,
as spirits that never die.

Michael Miley

Michael Miley

I'll Decide in the Middle of the Dream

There's a Y-shaped house at the end of my journey
with three long rooms open to the air.
I'm standing in the middle.

There's a window in each room at the end of each stem,
doorways at the junction, but without any doors.
A breeze is blowing through each of the rooms.

In the first room, which is blue, there's a wooden chair.
A leg of the chair is cracked down the middle.
A green praying mantis is sitting in the chair.

In the second room, which is red, there's a table with a bowl
resting on its surface, with black water pooled
in the bottom of the bowl.

In the third room, which is green, there's a ball rolling
on the hard stone floor,
moving slowly in the direction of the doorway.
The ball is yellow. A baby is crying.

The journey has been easy, almost like falling,
but whether I live or die
depends now upon the room that I enter,
and what I do in the room, once I do.

Michael Miley

The Songs of the Imaginals

Rising from sleep, this *hypnopompia*
is the Incubation of Dawn in the heart and the mind.
Clouds of congealed dream
breech like whales swimming towards Tortuga.
I float, still dazed, as the pod of sleek mammals,
fins flashing toward a brightening horizon,
baleen open to the sea,
comb countless krill into their mouths,
pink crustaceans feeding on plankton
floating in from another dimension.

I swallow the morning light like a cup of cream.
The Imaginals continue to rise on the quantum foam
breaking on the shores of my brain,
each figure a fractal that blooms
from the infinitely small to the humanly large,
from the contiguous presence of Space in all things,
from the open dynamo of Naught
within whose arms I swim
whenever I drop a fin of the Imagination
deep enough into the stream of my attention.

In the morning, the Imaginals are the plasmas of the Void,

jellyfish pulsing from the radiant Plenum.

At noon, they're the fivefold flowers of Light,

the sixfold symmetries of Mind-blown glass,

the *inner prisms* of everything I see.

At dusk, they're the geese that fly across the One Clear Sky

that everything shares, their haunting hound-like calls

dopplering from a vanishing wedge

that recedes into the descending Sun

towards which all things converge.

At night, they're the Fibonacci sequences

born of the Mind spiraling down,

the slow, ecstatic spin of galaxies *within*,

the heavenly conches blown by the Maya gods

as we walk together and sing

down the Long White Road

of the Dreamworld.

A Leaf Falls from the Tree of Knowledge

As I open the door to the bookstore, I'm suddenly standing in the hollow of a great tree, 'mid roots that house misshapen rooms, closets with red-green spotted doors, in a space easily forty feet across, lit by a blue-green phosphorescent glow. I go to the first door, which is narrow, but lumpy and leathery like the back of a frog, and open it and see it has a toilet inside, and I know suddenly that I have to pee, but if I go inside, it's so very narrow I won't be able to get out again, so I slam the door closed and hurriedly shuffle to the next one on the left. It's larger than the first, with the top of the door the shape of a broad man's shoulders. I know it's big enough for me, so I open it gingerly and in the green-blue glow of its interior I can see another toilet, so I almost go in, but I detect the sides of the room are shifting, they're beginning to squeeze, the door in my hand is changing its shape, like someone gripping the waist of a sandwich, so I know if I go in, the roots of the great tree will close around me and I'll never get out, so I hurriedly close that door and move on to the next.

When I open it, I see a small bald-headed man sitting inside, intent on his task, and he says *Hey hey! I'm already in here, go away! go away!* so I slam that door and as I turn into the space, I see that every root of the tree has a strange misshapen door on its inside, and the doors are arrayed in octagonal formation, each with a water closet within it, and as I look, some of the doors are opening, and strange staring men in 19th century clothing, with bowler hats and woolen long-coats, are emerging from the dark of the closets, looking for all the world like dazed dreamers painted by René Magritte. I know now I could go in and safely do my dastardly duty, but the prospect still frightens me, so I look up into the trunk of the tree for spiritual guidance and as I do, the space magically transforms into the huge used bookstore it was supposed to be, with a narrow metal spiral staircase in the center of the tree, winding endlessly to its upper floors, and tens of thousands of dusty old books piled up all around me.

The space is lit by beam of sunlight entering in through a window somewhere, fixed in its upper reaches, and in the descending amber light of the immense wood-paneled room, dust motes are drifting everywhere in the air. I step onto the spiral staircase, like Jack on his Beanstalk, and quickly climb upwards, occasionally looking down as I climb, watching the floor recede, with its books stacked up beneath me in huge disheveled piles.

At length, I come to a comfortable landing and step off the staircase and find myself browsing through the overflowing shelves, when I land on a thick pale paperback book by a *P. J. Somethingorother*, with a picture of a dazzling blond on the cover, as she lounges on a four-poster bed, a smirk on her face, in a tank top showing deep cleavage and a pleated skirt hiked above her knees.

As I open the book, I can hear the voice of New York critics who hail her tale in superior tones as *unlike any other*, an *impossibly clever satire* on the *endless parade of fools and scoundrels* that strut in abundance through the streets of their city.

It's a bawdy, brazen book, a montage of oddities that breaks all the rules, full of surreal pictures and scandalous disclosures, a scatological yet scholarly sibling to Julio Cortázar's survey of impossible things: *Around the Day in 80 Worlds*.

As I thumb through the pages, I can see quite plainly she has a terse, witty style, with very short sentences, unlike me, though many of the pages are nothing but pictures, so I return to the front of the book and now see an image the size of a full page, a surreal painting of a tall lanky figure in a long coat and top hat, suspended in midair, surrounded by a blue-green visible music, a spray of sounds hovering nearby, thick small bubbles with the texture of oil paint. He's a kind of Oscar Wilde of the Sky, falling from the Land of Giants, and as I look at him he comes alive, emerging from the page, which is a thin film that's somehow electronic, comprised of square pixels, but three-dimensional and holographic.

He begins to gossip in a confidential way, telling me a story of a huge country house and a family goblin and a dark and dank October night, alluding to cultic, forbidden sex among high society women, while a strange Schoenberg-like music is coming off the page, peeling off and evaporating in the air. I think, *it's incredible! What kind of book is this?* So I turn the page with the man who's falling and see that its surface is very thin, like an LCD screen, while its back is thick, taking up a third of the thickness of the book, it's something like a crystal version of the mechanism of a clock, with small gears turning and registers moving and the sound of infernal ticking, of Time running out, so I turn back to the page with the ranting figure, who's still going on with his bawdy story, which I barely understand, but I'm simply astonished at this 3D hologram that is alive and moving and talking to me, so I shout: *I simply, absolutely, MUST HAVE THIS BOOK!*

Then I turn around in a rush and begin to hurriedly descend the spiral staircase, brandishing the book as if it were a torch. As I do, I notice that the mountains of books are growing larger now and more encroaching, they're swelling and clustering so tightly around me that I can barely get down the staircase, so as I rush downwards in corkscrew fashion, I stumble momentarily on a corrugated step. With that, the book flies out of my hands, and I shout *OH NO!* as I watch it tumble in excruciatingly slow motion down a long narrow tunnel through the piles of books, twisting, turning, and tearing as it falls. I'm terrified I'll lose sight of it, so I rush down faster and faster, till I touch the bookstore's bottom, and then I'm suddenly there again in the chamber of toilets, so I rush over and yank open one of the doors, and there's the bald man I'd seen before, just getting up and pulling on his pants, dutifully flushing the toilet as he rises. I see him lean down and pick up a few pages, a torn folio of the mysterious book, which he holds now dumbly in front of him.

I simply, absolutely, must have that book! I shout again, as I grab at him for it, but he pulls it away and says, *Puleeese! Don't you have any manners? There's no need to shout! I KNOW what it is! It's one of those wonderful books by P. J. Somethingorother! Right? I daresay I've read almost everything she's written!*

But what's the NAME of this particular book? I continue to shout. *What's on its cover?!!*

Well, my friend, he says, while turning it over, *only a piece of it seems to have fallen down the spiral staircase. It tore itself up before it landed on my head and now, quite sadly, the cover is gone. But don't YOU remember the title? Was it* **Carumbulus of the Bitter Root***? That was a great book! I loved every minute of it!*

No No! I say. *It was something else!*

Was it **Perambulations Through the Red Warbulance***?* he continues, chewing his words, so I can barely understand him, while shuffling over to a pile of bookshelves, as I follow frantically behind.

No no! I cry. *It was some kind of satire on New Yorkers in heat, a kiss-and-tell story, with cultic overtones, told by the author and a falling man in a long-coat and top hat, complete with thousands of holograms and images, all of them with a capacity to move, to project themselves into space if I lingered but a moment on the page!*

Aha! he exclaims. *Then it must have been* **Wrangling with Quimly Behind the Spotted Shrooms***!* as he moves back further into the depths of the bookstore, scratching himself in his armpit as he goes, a bewhiskered smelly old man, balding and round-shouldered, pulling his reading spectacles from his pocket, but excited now at the prospect of selling me the book. Only now, he can't seem to find a copy of it, so he's down now sitting cross-legged on the floor, sorting and shuffling amidst the piles and piles, mumbling to himself, *It must be here! I saw it last week!* as he tosses the wrong books over his shoulders into the heaps of books behind him and continues his questioning.

*Was it **Pewter Corkscrew in the Sky**?* he continues, buried in his search.

No No! I say, feeling a mounting panic.

*Was it **Quintessence of Blue Spoons**?*

Ah no! I cry out, now feeling despair, as the image of the tumbling book spins down in front of me, my fingers outstretched, as if still hoping to catch it. *It's none of those, sir!*

Well, the least you could have done is READ THE TITLE, the bookseller grumbles. *How do you expect me to find it? P.J.'s incredibly prolific! She's written at least 10,000 books! Was it **Winkling in Whale Time**?* he continues, a plaintive tone now creeping into his voice.

And as he asks that question, I shake my head sadly and hear something stir outside the bookstore walls, as if someone is rubbing the trunk of the Great Tree, like the sound of a sigh of a ghost passing by, as the bookseller searches for an impossible Leaf fallen from The Great Tree of Knowledge—only to suddenly feel a pillow against my cheek, only to then feel the cool fall air blowing over me from the open bedroom door, only to inwardly cringe as I feel my mind now desperately reach to capture each fleeting leaf of evaporating scene, which even now begins to whisper away.

I know with cruel certainty that never again will I look on that book, never again see its living pages, with the Oscar Wilde-like falling figure, never again see its crystalline clockworks, or hear or see again its visible music peeling off the page, like pigment dancing before my eyes, unless I can somehow find a **Door of Return** in the side of the Tree, open it and dream the lucid dream I obviously require—to return one day and recover that book, that title, that leaf, from that Tree....

Michael Miley

Sketch for an Improbable Story:
Theseus and the Minotaur

This improbable story, which I may never write, is a tale of trauma, fragmentation of the self, and the painful creation of a unified identity. The trick will be to tell the story subjectively, (not like I'm doing now, using a lazy omniscient narrator), so the reader won't suspect the central fact until nearly the end: that Theseus Markides is a multiple personality; that his psyche is a maze, divided into separate, branching lifelines; that all the main characters in the story are him.

Now here's the backstory: In his childhood, Theseus was beaten repeatedly by his drunken father, a jobless plumber who knew how to use a pipe; while his mother became a streetwalker, just to make ends meet, so he's now like shattered glass. Resilient and creative in his shattering—the broken window panes, the shards of his abuse—Theseus appears at first to have four personalities, though there may be more.

There's Peter, who holds Theseus's culture and is intelligent and refined. He loves theater and music, but is a bit of a snob, though he's secretly attracted to whatever's taboo.

There's Bruno, who holds Theseus's anger and aggression. He's a dangerous thug who prowls around the streets at night, beating up punks he finds loitering in the panhandle of Golden Gate Park.

Then there's Erika, who lives for public display. She's a cross-dresser and works in a theater as a female impersonator. She loves to pretend she's a woman who loves men, though she's can't stand the thought of them touching her. She simply loves taunting them with the prospect of the forbidden. Only Erika suspects Bruno's existence: in her mind's eye, she's continually undressing in front of him. She knows that he hates her, but it's all part of the game of peek-a-boo, of hide-and-go-seek.

Then, of course, there's Theseus, who's confused and depressed, depleted by his alter egos, who holds all the wounding and must solve all the puzzles. So he's seeing a psychotherapist. She's peculiar in that she likes to knit during their therapy sessions. The presence of the ball of yarn, the act of knitting, is a symbol of what she does: she knits the garment of selfhood from the red yarn of love, working to recover his lost identity, where his being was whole, prior to his abuse. Her thread will guide Theseus out of his dark labyrinth and save him from the terrible Minotaur of self-destruction. It's a modern rendering of an old Greek myth. As you might suspect, her name is Ariadne.

Now here's the gist of the end of the story: His four alternate lives have gone their unmerry way. One dark night, in a cold November, in a drunken rage, while prowling about, Bruno kills a gangbanger in the Haight near the Panhandle and the gang sends a thug named Fritz out to get him. They've heard that Bruno's quirky, that he's been seen posing as a beefy girl in a small gay theater in the lower Castro. They're fired up by homophobic rage.

So the fates converge on a second dark night. In mid-December, Peter goes to a performance where Erika, the notorious female impersonator, performs the part of a hapless streetwalker. Peter attends the first act, then leaves, feeling sick, during intermission, only to black out in the theater hall. His subconscious knows he has to perform in the second act, so it's Erika who surfaces and enters the dressing room.

While she's getting dressed for her performance, with a blond wig, spike heels, and a slinky sequined dress, Fritz—our thug—sneaks into the theater through a backstage door. As the second act unfolds and Erika steps onstage in full regalia, Fritz is hiding in the wings, peeking out from behind a stage curtain.

Then the moment arrives: Erika is bending over to remove an ankle bracelet for one of her patrons, who is leering at her rump from a bed onstage. As Fritz aims his gun, Erika spies him out of the corner of her eye and from her cockeyed angle, flashes for a moment on the face of Bruno. She knows that Fritz has finally caught up with Bruno, so she pulls off one of her shoes and flings it at Fritz.

The long spike heel hits Fritz in the eye. As the gun goes off, now slightly deflected, the bullet grazes Erika's left shoulder, so she flings a second shoe at Fritz, striking him now in the forehead. Fritz goes down. Erika runs offstage. She flips into her Bruno persona and picking up a piece of pipe lying on the cold stage floor, pummels Fritz soundly, breaking his nose. Then Bruno tears off Erika's wig, though still in the sequined dress, wraps himself in a stage coat, and runs out barefoot into the street in a panic.

Bruno is terrified. The gang is clearly on his trail. In an acute anxiety attack, he flips back into Erika, ducks into the pool room of a nearby bar, and while listening to the clink of billiard balls, drinks herself into near oblivion, plying free drinks from the bartender, whom she knows. She then staggers home and falls into bed. She's so drunk she's already forgetting everything that's occurred as her head hits the pillow—except a soothing, romantic notion (which helps her fall asleep) that an elegant man named Peter, a fan of hers with erotic designs on her, had gone to see her in the play.

When he wakes, he's back to being Theseus. As he opens his eyes and looks around, he's perplexed by the sequined dress and stage coat on the floor. Did he bring someone home from the bar last night? If so, where is she? He also notices that his feet are filthy and a bit cut up and that his left shoulder has been bleeding and hurts like hell. He stands for an hour in the shower, washing the red wound, then suddenly remembers his appointment with his therapist. He bandages the shoulder, dresses quickly, and calls for a taxi. The next thing he knows, from his position on the couch, is that he's telling his therapist of a recurring dream, accompanied by a sense of impending doom.

The dream is always the same. He's attending some kind of Greek play. He suddenly finds himself onstage, wearing a woman's makeup and dress, when a Minotaur emerges from the maze of backstage curtains. When the Minotaur tries to kill him, he attacks the horned beast and nearly kills him in turn. Then he staggers off to a bar where he gets drunk, rejects an offer by a streetwalker of indeterminate sex, and stumbles back home. In the middle of his dream, his shoulder begins to hurt like hell, just as it does now, as if the Minotaur has bitten him, after whispering a terrible secret in his ear, something he's afraid to remember: *his true name.* But here comes the part that *really* frightens him: each time he dreams his dark dream, a woman in red emerges from a mirror, pulls out a gun, and shoots him through the heart. And then he wakes up.

Ariadne nods and sets down her knitting—which just happens to be a smock of twisted red yarn—then reaches for her notebook on the coffee table beside her.

Very interesting, she says, as she opens the notebook and clicks her ballpoint pen. *Since everyone in the dream is an aspect of you, we now know something very important: there are at least four personas in you, maybe more. The question now is: which is the real you? The dreamer, or one of the people you've dreamed? Or someone else, someone whole, who has not yet appeared?* As she scribbles in her notebook, he breaks down sobbing, hiding his face in his hands.

Just at that moment, the clock strikes four. The session is over. As Theseus weeps, feeling exposed, his personas now circling on a carousel in his head, Ariadne gets up, goes over to the couch, sits down beside them, and takes them in her arms.

The Cicada Eaters

When the drone of cicadas shatters the glass of a window in the cellar, winding through the dawn like the sound of a buzz saw, he slides in his dream on the surface of a shard, turning and mumbling as if chewing the sheets bunched against his lips, but the dream delves on, slipping downstream as cicadas keep landing, covering the roof and the porch and the windows of the house, till it stands there in the valley like a hapless shed taken over by vines. But when one of them crawls through an open window, fans silently to the bed, and lands on his forehead, he wakes as if he's been slapped in the face, then sits up abruptly, rubbing the fleeing nightmare from his eyes.

The room is quiet, not a cicada in sight, and the beams of late morning light lean like phantom carpentry from the windows to the floor.

With the plague still fresh in his mind, he rises slowly from the mattress, and careful not to awaken his wife, throws on his jeans and a rumpled shirt, and crossing the room with sleep still falling from his forehead, sits in the chair in front of his easel, placing a just-stretched canvas on the lip, and struggles to begin.

Mumbling *O Madre, what a terror I am to myself, let alone Manna,* he reaches for the tubes of green and brown and the largest brush, bending its bristles to unstiffen them, and begins right away on the fields near the house. With quick short strokes he defines the valley, the white picket fence surrounding the yard, and the outlines of the frame of the cabin—to prepare them for the innumerable wings, for the segmented bodies of brown and green, expanding and contracting with the strain of their flight, with an eye to where the cottonwoods stand, to where their feet will grip on the bark and the tender leaves will hang like tongues of parchment in the sun. And all of this will somehow rise from his dream of a doomed world, a world that is also the head of a woman and the face of a man, their bodies merged with the surrounding hills, the breasts of the woman hillocks of dry grass, the outline of her profile a range of mountains, his regal nose a promontory, his broad dark forehead a granite plateau, her sad curling lips the mouth of a canyon where the dogs are barking, where the voice of their children shriek in delight, out of the range of the invading swarm.

Manna, meanwhile, lies dozing on her side in the bed, stirring a bit as she pushes her arm through a small soft tunnel of sheets, her hand upturned like a starfish baking in the sun, when a cicada from his dream crawls onto her forehead and inches carefully down the bridge of her nose, bringing her slowly to the brink of sneezing. From the edges of sleep, her hand leaps up and her index finger rubs at her nostril like a child's eraser removing a monster. Then, turning on her back, she stretches and whispers, *Pablo, are you sleeping?* as she fans the sheet near her side, like a combine combing a field of wheat. But no one is there, so she drifts down through the furrows, pulling seeds from the tops of the stalks, till Pablo's dogs leap from his dream and chase her down the blackening rows, till the very last minute, right before they pounce, her real eye opens in fright and she spies her husband in the chair near the window, his movements creaking on the web of the wicker chair, the *tuff tuff tuff* of his brush dancing like a witch's hat on the canvas.

And the room swells with the odor of thinner, while a morning beam of light advances like a shard of glass across the floor.

Then, smiling to herself, over she goes, closing her eyes while she rolls and pulls the sheet to one side, so that a long warm stretch of thigh appears like a dune on a salty shore where Pablo and the children play, cupping the sand for castles threatened by the afternoon tides. Then over she goes again, flat on her back, her knee like an island rising in the green, her breasts now poking through scarves of water, her pert soft nipples the miniature castles where Pablo plays, singing on Sundays a popsicle music in the heat of summer, while washing his mouth of sand he sips at the sea, sucking up shrimp that swim through his eyes and ears and shimmer 'round Manna, beautiful Manna, who sleeps and dozes, rises and does not rise, who hears the *tuff tuff tuff* of a brush as if he's shaking devils from a witch's hair, while she whispers *Pablo, poquito Pablito,* and he answers *Manna, O monkey's banana, you see me here darling, painting away, will you ever rise?*

But she doesn't rise and an hour passes and Manna sleeps and Pablo paints and the blade of sun moves over his foot like a knife of light and the stirs and sighs of Manna drift like seahorses through the coves of the pillows, sunk in the deep like sounding whales, where the fish need lights on the ends of their noses just to find their way.

Now Pablo is painting the sunlit porch on the edge of the field, where cicadas begin to overrun the wheat, and he reaches for the umber and ash, clotting the furrows with their leaflike bodies, with their chitinous shells clinging to the trees, their pink-tan color like the tails of shrimp, then he reaches too for the tan and brown for the pods of catalpa, while a gentle wind kicks up outside, kissing the bowl where Pablo and Manna are flexing their gills, goldfish breathing in the depths of a cove, bubbles rising from their puckering mouths as they watch from below for flies or skeets on the tensile surface of the sky, gaping in wonder at the hot noon sun burning overhead.

And the blue of the room is suspended there, with the *tuff tuff tuff* of Pablo's brush, in a light that lingers on the surface of the roof as the eastern region of sky grows dark.

Pablo is painting rapidly now, the picket fence taking shape 'round an empty corral, a chicken scratching in the dust of the yard, when a swarm of cicadas flows from his brush to the eastern sky, a curved, sharp blade of darkening cloud, his mind now in awe—as in Flammarion's print of the medieval world, with the Sun and Stars, the Moon and a man, on one side of an arc, and wheels and clouds turning and drifting on the other side of the arc, as his head pokes through, wide-eyed and wondering at the hidden machinery beyond the edge of the World, where Heaven and Earth meet.

As a blackened finger of cicada leaches down on a distant hill, to the left in the canvas where the cows are grazing, the tips of the mountains to the west and right are leached of gold by the start of an eclipse that already halfway darkens the sun. Still, the valley in the middle is bright, with the small house there with its porch of pine, while the soft *tuff tuff* of a few stray cicadas now pelting the house make Pablo pause and listen for a moment, then chuckle to himself at the tricks of the mind. He resumes his task, focusing now on the logging road that winds like rope into the amber mountains, past the poplars poised like fearful soldiers, standing still though they wish they could run.

And the barking of the dogs has a different tone now, shriller and more urgent, as they jump and run through the canyon hollow, circling and worrying in anxious circles, bounding and baying to where the children are running and splashing in the stream. The boy laughs loudly at the schools of trout zipping like nervous skaters in the shallows. He picks up stones, the round red ones with speckles of blue and the square gray ones of chiseled granite, and plunks them clumsily into the stream, in hopes of bopping the trout on their noses, while they scatter in fifteen different directions. His sister, meanwhile, has left the stream, is picking dandelions on the slope of a hill, smelling them deeply as she pulls them from the ground, when she's lost for a moment in a dandelion world, where an ant is making its way up and down through the petals of yellow, an armored conqueror exploring the New World. Then the dogs tumble into the stream below, whining and barking at the palpitating air, startling the boy as frolic and bark, so that he drops his stones at his feet, while the girl turns quickly also, dropping her handful of flowers on the ground. Then they both look up and away. As they watch the sky in the distance darken, a flock of birds makes off from the trees in the direction of the dark. Light begins to leach from the sky and a wind whips up smelling of chewed grass, and off in the fields there's a lowing of cows, and suddenly the dogs are nowhere to be seen. As the fish begin roiling in the stream and the boy feels the air go cold, he hears it now, for the very first time: a winding drone, like a saw from the farm, rising and falling in the hot summer air. And at the sound of the drone, the girl starts to weep, fearful of her fate....

Meanwhile, Manna's voice comes faint and coaxing, drifting from the bed like smoke, as Pablo's brush goes *tuff tuff tuff* and the sound is mirrored in a *tuff tuff* noise now hitting the porch. Then Manna mumbles, distracting him now with her whispering voice: *O my heart, what is it, sweetheart? What's out there, Pablo, where the children are playing?* And then, quite sharply: *Where are you, Pablo? Are you still painting there? Come to me now!* as she moans and drifts in the bed through her scarves, clicking her tongue on the roof of her mouth, so that Pablo is roused at the moist soft sound even as he paints. So down goes his brush, as he pushes his chair back and stands and stretches, lingering a moment before the glistening canvas, gazing intently at the small, dark figure peering from the window of the half-painted cabin.

It's the figure of a man sitting near an easel, painting his own painting of a cabin and an easel and a man who is painting, while outside a storm of wings is gathering....

Then he lumbers to the bed, shedding his jeans and his paint-smeared shirt, as he dives down naked into the soft warm green like a seal dipping his whiskers in the waves, down to the coral reefs where a dream of Manna is chasing a school of silver minnows. Then an eel shoots out from the coral, encircling his neck, while the leg of an octopus slides over his thigh, entwining with his, till he feels the warm damp mollusk down there, sucking gently against his outer thigh. *There you are, you scruffy monkey!* she whispers into his ear, tousling his hair. *You've been a busy boy, now haven't you, Pablo? You smell like oil paint. Ambitious and obsessed, even on Sunday! Leaving your poor Manna to her horrible dreams of plagues and cicadas. You must be punished!* Then she grabs his cock and yanks it gently and reaches round and pinches his buttock. And he laughs, but wonders, *Is it possible for two to dream the same dream? Or was my dream just a shadow of hers?* while nibbling her ear as if foraging now for the net of all sound, nosing there among the strands of her hair entangling his face like drifting kelp.

Then he nibbles downshore to the darker beds, the musky coves and pockets and cups, nuzzling the mussel fixed in the crook, till she's all around him now, smothering his face with the belly of a seal. Then he makes his journey upshore again, nosing nimbly in search of new shells, past the darker inlets where the pipers run, nibbling nimbly as he passes the grass, the bread of Manna rising in the heat, when suddenly their tongues are wrestling together, groping blindly in the barnacled caves where language is born, rooting for words that taste like fruits when you bite them, while the cells of their bodies, like schools of endangered fish, are swirling much faster now, swirling much faster now. She murmurs *Pablo* and he whispers *my love* and the tensile surface of the pond grows rough, while the house around them trembles with the *tuff tuff tuff* of something like rain. A moan begins in her throat, a foghorn barely audible at first, rising gradually on the edges of sound, warning the fishermen of hidden reefs, but he's feeling for them now with his pole, nudging the sponges where anemones surge, till the water breaks over their skin and her voice now rises in his ear like a tongue of the sea, crying *Pablo, O my love, my darling!* while Pablo moans *O Manna, my life, my beautiful wife!* as the foam rushes down upon them and they roll into a knife of light cutting its way on the surface of the shore.

Then they rest awhile, as the sea tongues lick their limbs and the tide subsides. Manna sighs and murmurs *Pablo, poquito Pablito, where are the children? Are they outside playing?* And Pablo answers: *Yes, my sweet, they're outside romping around with the dogs. They were down by the river the last time I looked.* And then he rolls to her flank and clings there a moment, tucking his head into the kelp on her shoulder, while they both drift down into the dampened sheets and off into the land of breath and wings.

Now the breeze deepens through the open window, and the curtains billow toward the center of the room, when the first one lands on the sill with a *tufflike* sound, then crawls and wanders along the window's ledge, launching itself into the center of the room, fanning out past the billowing drapes to where the lamp on the nightstand sits. It lands there now with a *tuff* of small feet, crawls awhile on the rim of the shade, then down it goes on the taut inner surface. For a moment, it's out of sight, but then down it flits to the headboard of the bed. Then another one lands on the sill, then two more are crawling on the wall, and then Manna rolls on her back, pulling the sheets weakly around her, damp but warmed by the dying sun, while Pablo rolls on his back in her shadow, his arm now sliding beneath the sheets in search of her skin, till it finds her thigh and clings there hopefully, like a starfish dreaming of land and sky. Then one of them drops right down with a *tuff*, scrambling there on the edge of her pillow and crawls teetering into her hair, making its way onto a tangled strand, while Pablo's mouth opens a bit and a snore begins low at the back of his throat. Then two more land on the pillows, near the dark damp currents rising so sweetly from the depths of their lungs, floating up like the mists of language, a faint steam rising from the mouth of Manna, a geyser fuming from the mouth of Pablo. Wings and feet are perched and poised on the brink of both wells, till they dip down softly and disappear within, sipping like thieves at the moist soft tongues where the voice of love first finds its way. And as the small wingéd bodies descend into the room, the *tuff tuff tuff* of a brush or feet are the only sounds on the shingles of the roof, on the dark, doomed canvas, on the darkening surface of the sheets....

Michael Miley

Embarking in Eidoland

We'll meet again in a place of no wind
and our speech will be the sound of petals dropping,
phonetic ash of a disappearing tongue.
And I will be encumbered by my eyes,
till you take them gently from me
and give me prisms from your travelling pouch.
Then from some private mirage of mizzle and shoal,
you'll launch for me a skiff in which we'll drift,
the purling waters pretense of a motion
auguring some destination.
For we'll have arrived,
arbored in the baffling sense
of having known one another—
before our desires, like ships of war
had crossed the seas
and quartered the horizon.

Ellie Portner

The Muse

she is fickle
she does not meet commitments
nor give assurances
time for her has no boundaries

sometimes
she withdraws
and I am afraid
she will not return

I tempt her back
with whispered promises
I do not keep

I do not trust her
the one who shares my solitude
who comes to me
to fill the empty places

Summer

A couple of days
Went missing last week
It didn't really matter
They were summer days
Too hot for thinking
Too lazy for work

Wind too weak to unsettle
The dead oleander blossoms
Browning on the concrete

My days ride a carousel
Round and round
Up and down
Silence rides with me
When it ends
The emptiness comes
There was no journey
No fond memories
The ticket stub
Is a kitchen calendar
With circled entries

In the evening
Ceiling fan rotating
Temperature dropping
I become aware
That another day is gone
Summer will end soon

In the meantime
Tall glasses of un-sweet tea
Sweat into puddles
My watercolors wait on the desk
A stack of tax papers
Wait on the dining room table
The world of my creation
Waits for me to enter it again
But I am not ready

Ellie Portner

Little Fox

Come home little fox
It is near morning light
You have been gone
All through the night
You are too young
To be hunting alone
It is better to wait
Until you're full grown

Do you stand in the night
Watch and listen – then
Leap high in the air?
Come straight down

Land on your feet
To pin a wee mouse
Under there?

Or are you asleep
On a soft bed of leaves?
Is your tail curled
Under your nose?
Are you warm and safe?
Are you dreaming tonight
Of little fox friends and foes?

Come home little fox
Your vixen is worried
She is waiting for you
Run back home
To the den little pup
Before the morning dew

The Skunk

I am a skunk – a little chunk
No bigger than a cat
When I stomp, stomp, stomp
On my flat front feet
It is time for you to scat
Cause when I am scared – I am the worst
You do not want to scare me first
Go away – leave me alone
I do not like strangers near my home

When I stomp, stomp, stomp
I am warning you
Do you know what skunks can do?
If I turn around – beware
When my tail is in the air
It means that I am going to spray
You will be stinky for a day

When I stomp, stomp, stomp
On my flat front feet
Hurry away – while you still smell sweet

Ellie Portner

If . . .

an empty paper bag
soiled and torn
no longer
can you hold
anything
for me

I reach inside
your paper shell
and feel
the shadow
of what used to be

if you were a paper kite
I would hold your string
and we could fly

Ellie Portner

Millet

I am a small bird
Perched on your shoulder
I lick the salt from your skin
You smell of millet
I lean against your warm moist neck
Rest my head under my wing
And sleep

When you speak I awake
You let me drink
The water in your mouth
That rises from
The fountain of your life
But I taste only millet

Eve

Eve waits eyes closed
Under her apple tree
Blossoms shade her face
She breathes their fragrance

Later she will claim
Her right to the apples
She who watched them grow
Felt their life within the blossoms
As a mother of a child
As the goddess of trees

If there are no apples
Because there was too much rain
Or not enough

Because they were destroyed
By insects and birds

Because she did not gather
Those that fell to the ground
Thinking she could wait until
Their rosy perfection hung ripe
On branches within her reach

Eve is patient
Her tree will bear apples
In their season
Apples she will share
With whomever she pleases

Ellie Portner

Adobe Road

After the rain
The land is green and yielding
The air – heavy, gray and sweet

I walk the eastern hills
My leather sandals
Soaked with rainwater
My arms swing free
My tread gentle on the rise

In one breath
I reach beyond the hills
Today I am a giant

Ellie Portner

The Walls Are Closing In

I awake in a room
The blue of a stormy day
When cloud cover
Blocks the sun
And there are no shadows

I awake to strangers
Standing close together
As if they were
A gathering of horses
Under a hot sun
Enclosed behind barbed wire
In a field of dead grasses

Blue fills my ears
And I cannot hear
The keening voices
In this room of strangers

Ellie Portner

Cauliflower

In My Dreams #3

Some time ago
I stored three large fresh
Plastic wrapped
Cauliflower heads
On the shelf in the hall closet
It had been long enough
For me to have forgotten
That they were still there

The odor of rotting vegetable
Reminded me
Of the neglected cauliflower
I opened the closet door
I reached for a cauliflower head

My fingers did not feel
The expected bumpy shape
My ears did not hear
The crinkle of plastic
I felt a small soft body
I felt velvety human skin
I carefully removed
The warm thing from the shelf
And stared with disbelief
Into sleepy black eyes
Of a dirty naked boy child

Ellie Portner

I held him to my chest
And was rewarded with his soft sigh
He circled his arms around my neck
And pressed his knees into my body
I felt a mother's heart beat inside me

I had no idea
What I was going to do
With this small child who had
Grown from a cauliflower

I retrieved the empty plastic
Cauliflower wrapper from the shelf
And carefully read
The entire label twice
But there were no instructions
Nor any information
To help me deal with this issue

Call of the Sea

1.
The sea calls to me
It has wrapped me in
Invisible strands
To hold me close
It tells me I have returned
And we must be together

2.
The sea brings me waves
One after the other to seduce me
It calls the sun to warm its waters
That I may bathe in comfort
At sunrise and sunset
It paints its surface
So that I will never
Leave these shores
But wait patiently each day
To praise its creations

3.
The sea lures me
With soaring Pelicans
Nesting Ospreys
And small birds hunting prey
In freshly moistened sand
Along its shores

4.
I am a victim of its persuasion
I am found in the pleasures
Of living on the shore
I am a child of water

Dawn

The fading moon
Has lost its right
To remain in the sky
The horizon
Welcomes a yellow sun
I embrace the song
Of sea, wind and birds
Dawn comes
As a promise

Take Me with You

Take me with you
I want to be a passenger
On your flying machine
To fly far away
From this inky darkness

Your guardian
Has refused me passage
And there is no room
In my dreaming
To ask elsewhere

Paint the sky
With an amber trail
That I may follow
I will always be other
In this inky darkness

The Soprano

1.
The soprano visited
At sunset last evening
She does not come to sing
As often as I would like
But when she emerges
Her notes float effortlessly
From her mouth
Filling my heart with her music

2.
I do not know why she is reticent
Nor when she will visit
I cannot coax her with songs
Nor bribe her with warm liquids
Perhaps it is because the alto
Does not tolerate intruders
And spitefully guards
Her musical territory

3.
The alto was singing
When the soprano
Suddenly took over
She spent the rest
Of the evening
Singing each song
As if it were her last
Until she tired
Took her bows
And left me again

Feathers

Feathers adrift
From an old flat pillow
That had cradled
Too many heads
And is now
Without purpose
The feathers
Found their way out
Through invisible holes
In a fabric
That had lost
The will to hold them

When I Am

when I cannot hear
I am seduced by silence
and become my mind

when I cannot see
I abandon my mind
and become my body

when I lose my hair
I will wear a hat
and become a spy

Helen Rowntree

Helen Rowntree

A Burial in El Salvador

The year was 1940 and I was eleven years old. The bus from San Salvador had brought Mother and me to Santa Tecla to attend my uncle Miguel Angel's funeral. It was the first time I had ever been to a funeral. Miguel Angel had died three days earlier and the small adobe house was filled with *familia y amigos* who had come from various towns and villages to attend the wake and interment. The oppressive, tropical heat was suffocating and intensified bodily odors as well as the cloying smell of gardenias. The front room had been cleared of most furnishings and a small altar had been erected against the main wall. A large photo of Miguel Angel hung amid many religious pictures. The closed casket, a simple wooden box, had been placed in front of the altar, surrounded by candles and vases filled with fresh lilies and gardenias.

In the small kitchen, women were busy tending to the continuous meal they had begun preparing two days before. The wood-burning stove was covered with pots of beans, rice and tamales, and the air was filled with the pungent aromas of cumin, bay leaf, garlic and cinnamon. Pitchers of *horchata* and *aguas frescas* were placed on a small table near the front door to welcome the thirsty travelers. Out in the yard, a whole pig was roasting on a spit and would be eaten after we returned from the cemetery. In those days, the poor waked their dead at home, did not have them embalmed, and by law, had to bury the body within three days.

At three o'clock, Father Lorenzo came to conduct the funeral service. Everyone crowded into the front room as he blessed the children and comforted the widow. Then he moved to the small altar and stood in front of the coffin, where he began the ceremony. He chanted the Latin prayers while swinging his aromatic censer over the casket: to the left and to the right, to the left and to the right. The ritual was hypnotic and the smoke from the censer lingered in the air, hovering over the bereaved.

After the ceremony, six men, brothers and cousins, lifted and carried the casket outside, and placed it on a cart to be pulled by two oxen. The two oxen were as much family as everyone else and, as I looked into their sad eyes, I thought they knew that their master had died. Then, carrying the lilies and gardenias to place over the grave, all the relatives and friends gathered behind the wagon, walking in a solemn procession to the cemetery.

A light rain had fallen during the last hour and the air felt humid and filled with the smell of moist dirt. The casket shook as the wagon lumbered down the stony road, sometimes sinking into a muddy hole, sometimes stopping while someone removed a large rock that impeded progress.

We arrived at the cemetery, which felt peaceful, its old crooked tombstones placed haphazardly over the grassy lawns. Small pots filled with flowers leaned against them and the trees were filled with happy, chirping birds, oblivious to the sad proceedings taking place below. To my surprise, some of the men began digging up my grandmother's grave. I could hear the thud of the shovels as they hit the stony earth, then dumped the dirt in neat piles around the grave. Mother then explained to me that it was not unusual to bury more than one person in the same grave, so Miguel Angel was going to be buried with my grandmother. Presently, the digging stopped. I heard the men murmuring; they had found my grandmother's casket and were removing her bones, which they wrapped reverently in a black shawl to place them inside Miguel Angel's coffin.

The priest resumed his prayers, once again swinging his censer over the grave. I knew what was coming, so I quickly ran to hide behind a nearby tree, about fifty feet away.

Then they opened the casket, thereby releasing the overpowering stench of putrefaction. The smell of death floated up the little hill where I stood shaking behind a tree. The odor in the air seemed to permeate everything: the trees, the bushes, the hills, all the way up to the clouds. I felt I would never be able to escape this terrible smell . . . it would follow me everywhere, forever.

Overcome by fear and the horrible odor, I didn't know what to do or where to run. So I pulled my shawl down over my head and face, and trying not to breathe, I threw myself on the ground burying my face in the tall, sweet-smelling grass.

The Piano

I have always appreciated my husband Bob's generosity and sense of humor, but sometimes, his humor could get out of hand. I remember once when it could have landed him in jail.

Bob pulled this particular prank when we were still living in Park Ridge, Illinois, in the old, large, red brick house that was at that time filled to capacity with family. Because of various catastrophes, mishaps and misfortunes, our whole family was living together: my mother who had suffered a stroke, her caregiver Louisa, my two sons Mike and Tom, my daughter Susi and her husband Adrian and their two small boys, Philip and Miles, not to mention Bob and I — all packed in together like socks in a drawer.

Life of late had been very difficult for Susi and Adrian, and that day was their fifth wedding anniversary, so Bob and I decided to treat them to a celebration. The four of us dressed up in our best party clothes and set out for Café la Tour, an elegant French restaurant in Oakbrook. We started by ordering champagne and raising our glasses in honor of their anniversary. We then ordered hors d'oeuvres and more champagne. A wonderful meal followed, which I still remember to this day, beginning with Medallions of Veal Pierre, and ending with Soufflé Grand Marnier — and of course, more champagne. By this time we were all feeling quite mellow and didn't want the festivities to end, so on the way home, Susi suggested we end the evening by stopping at the disco in the Marriott Hotel, not far from home.

It was about 1:00 a.m. when we pulled into the hotel parking lot. The disco was very popular with the younger crowd and was located on the opposite side of the front entrance to the building, so we had to walk quite a distance down a long windowed corridor to get to it. On the way, Susi noticed a baby grand piano in a corridor outside one of the party rooms and stopped to admire it.

"Gee whiz! Look at this *beautiful* piano. I've always dreamed of owning one of these. I wonder why it's just sitting here in the hall. It looks completely abandoned!"

We continued down the hall and entered the disco, which was filled to the rafters with young people dancing. The disco, decorated in a 1950s style, sported half of a 1955 Chevy mounted high on the wall behind the bar. The music was loud and frantic, so Adrian and I, who were not good dancers, let Susi and Bob do the dancing for us. It was nearly 2:00 a.m. when we decided we'd had enough drinking and dancing and we'd best head for home.

Walking down the long corridor toward the parking lot, we again encountered the baby grand piano. Susi cuddled up to it and began petting it as though it were a house cat. *"My goodness!* This lovely piano is still out here in the hall! Isn't someone going to *put it in a room*? It looks *abandoned* here! I can't believe no one is concerned about it! *I sure wish this piano were mine!"*

No sooner had she said this than Bob sidled up to her, the devil in his smile: "How would you like to *have* this piano, Susi? I bet we could take it *home* with us and nobody would even miss it!" Both Bob and Susi had a penchant for swiping silverware from fancy restaurants. If truth be told, they were a couple of kleptos.

"What? Are you serious?" Susi gasped. "You would take this piano home for me? How would you do that?"

"Just leave it to me and give me a hand here!" Adrian and I just looked at him aghast.

"What? You two chickens don't want to help? Okay, Susi, it's up to you and me." And with that, they began pushing the piano down the hall toward the parking lot.

"Wait a minute!" I raised my hand. "Just what do you two think you're doing? Someone will see you moving that piano and you'll both be in serious trouble!" Adrian and I were alarmed, even though we were laughing.

Susi and Bob continued, unperturbed. They pushed it down the hall, a serious, purposeful expression on their faces. They moved resolutely past hotel guests, past the main lobby and the front desk, past waiters, maintenance workers and maids. No one paid any attention to them except to get out of their way to let them pass. Seeing Bob in his dark suit and bow tie and Susi in her long party dress, no doubt everyone thought they were a piano player and singer, hired for one of the lounges or private parties. But because they were clearly so serious about stealing the piano, Adrian and I decided to disassociate ourselves from the two drunken lunatics and went outside to the sidewalk paralleling the corridor leading to the parking lot. We could still see them through the windows as they continued down the hall and watched incredulously as two housemen moved their vacuum cleaner and supplies cart to let them pass.

When they finally reached the end of the corridor, they encountered a revolving door. When Bob tried unsuccessfully to open it wide, one of the housemen graciously opened the door for him and helped him push the piano out onto the canopied sidewalk leading to the parking lot.

Bob was jubilant. "They're *so helpful* at this hotel! Now . . . if we can just push this piano across the street to the gas station, we can hide it behind that big sign and see if we can get Mike to come with his van and pick it up. Between all of us we should be able to load it onto the van and take it home."

With that, he went to the pay phone and dialed our house. Our son Michael, awakened from a sound sleep, answered the phone. Bob told him to get up and bring his van over to the gas station at Higgins and Cumberland, because soon we would have a baby grand piano there and we needed the van to take it home.

"Are you kidding?" he asked incredulously. "You guys must be drunk!"

"Well, we've had a few, but this is for real. The piano is beautiful and it's a present for Susi!"

"Wow! The kleptos strike again! Unfortunately, it won't work. I outfitted my van with a bed and a bookshelf. There's no way a baby grand piano will fit in it." But getting into the spirit of the moment, Mike suggested, "Why don't you call Tom Steinbach? He has a pick-up truck and has always been sweet on Susi. He's crazy enough to help you. Here's his number."

Bob then called Steinbach. "Are you guys nuts?" he answered sleepily over the phone. "There's no way in hell I'm going to get out of bed in the middle of the night to help two lunatics steal a piano!"

"Okay! If you don't want to do it, we'll think of something else!" Bob hung up and faced Adrian and me.

"JUST A MINUTE!" I said, totally alarmed. "You've taken this caper far enough!!! Do you want to go to jail? How will the local newspaper headlines read tomorrow? 'Vice President of local computer software company caught stealing piano from Marriott Hotel.'" A sheepish grin came over his face and Susi started to laugh hysterically. Soon we were all laughing. We left the piano under the canopy, climbed into the car, and drove home.

As soon as we entered the house, Bob went to the phone and called the Marriott.

"Hello? I'd like to speak to the night manager, please." Pause — and more laughter. "Hello? Is this the night manager? Well I'd like to tell you we had a *swell* time at the disco tonight, but I'd also like to say I don't think much of your internal security. Why? Well, if you go out onto the sidewalk leading to the parking lot, you'll find a baby grand piano sitting out there all by its lonesome. We were going to take it home, but the two ladies with us weren't strong enough to help us lift it onto the truck, though perhaps we could have asked your night workers for help, they were so accommodating. When we wheeled the piano down the hallway they even opened the revolving door wide so we could get the piano through the door. No, no, I'm *not* crazy! Go check it out for yourself. And you'd better hurry. They're predicting rain tonight. In fact, it was just starting to sprinkle when we walked into our house."

When Bob hung up the phone, we all dissolved into laughter, and finally decided it was time to go bed.

Helen Rowntree

My Mother's Hands

Soft, small hands dipped in henna.
Skin, like dried rose petals,
fragile as the membrane of an eggshell.
Palms, pumiced smooth
by the stones of toil and caring.
Veins and wrinkles, recording all the years
of doing and praying.
Blunt-cut nails, round and flat,
ridged, thin as tissue paper, never manicured.
Cooking, cleaning, and medicating hands.
Comforting hands that dried tears.
Gentle hands that braided hair,
that mended, embroidered, picked flowers.
Strong hands that chopped wood,
wrung chicken necks, plucked feathers.
But, oh . . . that was so long ago.
Now your hands lie across your breast,
no longer fluttering,
no longer picking imaginary lint off your quilt,
no longer reaching out to touch a transparent face
that floats above your bed.
The silver rosary lies still in your hands,
its beads no longer slipping through your fingers.
Soon the dried petals of your skin will crumble,
turn into delicate, sweet smelling dust.
Small, motionless hands, dipped in henna,
soon to be one with the soft, brown earth.

The Weeping Quilt

I saw you hanging on the white museum wall,

drooping and sagging, faded and torn,

quite ugly, in fact – uneven and worn.

So why did you catch my eye?

I had glanced quickly at your companions,

quite fetching in their colorful patches,

snatches of different fabrics,

stitched together into whimsical patterns.

But somehow, they didn't touch me, so I quickly moved on.

And then I saw you – quiet, ugly and wretched.

As I stood before you, I thought I heard you moan,

in a deep, dark Negro voice.

Was that Lutisha moaning?

Lutisha had created you out of old britches and shirts,

worn out by the man she loved,

the man who gave her nine children and nothing more.

Lutisha's days were filled with toiling in the fields,

picking cotton, growing vegetables,

washing the little ones, cooking the meals.

Then, finally at dusk, she sat by the kerosene lamp,

and worked on you.

Her arthritic, brown hands fashioned you lovingly,

filling in the holes with unmatched scraps,

turning the edges, stitching around them tightly,

'till the holes became the dark windows of your soul.

Tell me, did you lie gently at night,

over their entwined bodies?

Were you in attendance when the children were born?

Did you warm and comfort Lutisha after he left?

But now Lutisha has died and you are in mourning,

fading from denim blue to pale bone.

Your stitches have come undone,

and the cotton batting inside you has dropped.

Your fragile, wrinkled skin now hangs loose.

You hang wretched and drooping like aging flesh.

Bagging and sagging like an old woman's eyes,

like an old woman's eyes when they fill with tears.

Thoughts on "Bar" a quilt by Lutisha Pettway, circa 1950
From the Quilts of Gee's Bend Exhibit
De Young Museum 2006

Illuminated Balloons

The world of private clubs was entirely different from any of the many worlds I had ever been exposed to. I had been selected from a very small group of women in the food service and hospitality field to manage one of the most exclusive women's clubs in the Chicago area. Its members have always been exceptionally accomplished women in their own right, and many are the wives and daughters of the principals of major corporations, banks and law firms. They reside primarily on the Gold Coast or the North Shore suburbs. The imposing eight-story building is located on Michigan Avenue's Magnificent Mile, in the premier business district of the city. It is an elegant building, both inside and out, from the mansard roof and wrought iron trim, to the two-story reception room on the second floor, and the two-story oval ballroom on the seventh.

The women I met there were elegant, refined and pleasant. Some were fun, talented and very intelligent. However, for me, there was one member that stood out from all the rest, who possessed all these qualities and more, and that was Miss Hooper. Frances Hooper was a maiden lady of eighty-five when I met her, and I was immediately captivated by her twinkling eyes and no-nonsense demeanor. Over the years, we became friends and Bob and I were privileged to be invited to some of her gatherings. Each year at Christmas time, she gave an extravagant party at the women's club, and this morning, she was meeting with me to plan this year's event. She was inviting sixty-four of her "most intimate friends" and was all excited about it.

"Mrs. Rowntree, I want to have a spectacular main entree, a spectacular dessert and spectacular decorations." This was typical Miss Hooper hyperbole, but she meant just that.

When she walked into my office that morning, she was smiling excitedly and had more than the usual twinkle in her eyes.

"Everything is falling into place. Wait 'till I tell you what I've planned by way of entertainment. I am really pleased about it all."

"Come in. Come in. I want to hear all about your plans and surprises." I loved working with her.

Miss Hooper was about five feet tall, stooped from osteoporosis, with sparse, reddish-gray hair. She was intelligent, witty, creative, happy — and very wealthy. She was a self-made woman and was proud to let everyone know she had begun her own advertising business while still in her twenties. She could be difficult, cantankerous, very charming, and I loved her.

"First, I must take off these abominable shoes. Why don't they make shoes that are good-looking *and* comfortable. I always have to decide whether I want to look stylish or feel comfortable. Ah! That's better!

You can't guess what I'm planning to have as entertainment. I've found a couple of charming dancing girls and a seamstress who has agreed to make harlequin costumes for them. Doesn't that sound great?"

"Absolutely! How do you plan to feature them?"

"Well, I thought we could put long tables in a large square around the Silver Room, leaving an opening at each corner for the dancers to come into the center of the square, each carrying in a spectacular dessert which they would present to each table. Then they will do their dance. I have engaged a very nice trio of musicians, so we must be sure the piano is tuned. I want the main entrée to be the club's famous individual cheese soufflés, accompanied by fresh asparagus and a lovely green salad. Now all we need is a spectacular dessert. What can you suggest?"

I recited a number of the Club's specialties which she kept rejecting, saying: "No. No. That's not spectacular enough." Finally, really going out on a limb, I suggested we make a croquembouche for each table. I didn't even know if the kitchen staff could make such a thing, but I knew they always came through, no matter how demanding the request.

"What is that?"

I found a picture of a croquembouche in one of my cookbooks and showed it to her. She squinted, her tiny eyes, peering closely at the picture, and then she exclaimed: "That's it! That's it! We don't need to look any further! This dessert is certainly spectacular enough, but it must be decorated for Christmas. Can you do that?"

"Of course we can," I said, taking my life in my hands, thinking of what Miss Rhynsburger, our kitchen manager, would say when she got the menu. The tiny cream puffs filled with Bavarian cream were no problem. The syrup to hold them together was another matter.

"Well, that's settled. Now let's talk about decorations. I'm renting little gold Venetian chairs and I want everyone seated only on one side of the table, so they can all see the dancers. I want lots of red and gold poinsettias and lastly I want illuminated balloons around the room."

"Illuminated balloons? I don't think I have ever seen illuminated balloons. I haven't the slightest idea where I can find them."

"Mrs. Rowntree, you have always come through for me before, so I'm sure you will be able to get them."

Right! And so began my quest for illuminated balloons.

I called the usual party decorating services without success. I tried costume and prop stores to no avail. Finally, on a hunch, I called the Goodman Theater, which usually puts on wonderful plays for children, and they suggested I call Jack Frost, a company that provided decorations and props for their events.

"Illuminated balloons? No problem." They would provide thirty large illuminated balloons and set them up in the Silver Room. Bingo! I heaved a sigh of relief.

Then my phone rang. It was the kitchen. "Mrs. Rowntree? Ione Rhynsburger here. May I come up to discuss Miss Hooper's menu with you?"

"Certainly. Come right now if you wish."

To say that Miss Rhynsburger intimidated me under the best of circumstances was an understatement. Miss Rhynsburger was a small, serious-minded woman in her late sixties. She was also a meticulous chef and ran her kitchen impeccably. Everyone respected her and feared her. Asking her to produce eight croquembouches for a special Miss Hooper luncheon while still having to put out the daily luncheon for the dining room was downright suicidal.

Miss Rhynsburger came in, and when I looked at her, I knew immediately that I was in deep doodoo.

"Mrs. Rowntree. I haven't made a croquembouche in forty years. Furthermore, the bakers have *never* made a croquembouche, which means I will have to nurse them through the whole process. As you know, making the syrup that holds the whole thing together is a very difficult thing to do, and we need to do it that morning — not the day before and not for *one* croquembouche, but for *eight*. I'm not very happy about this." Then she smiled slyly. "Perhaps you can come down that morning and give us a hand."

Now she had me. I had *never* made a croquembouche in my life and she knew it.

The day of the event came. I went in at seven in the morning and we started working to get the syrup the right consistency — not too runny, since it needed to hold the tiny cream puffs together, and not so hard that it would break your teeth. After about five tries, we had it! We began stacking the cream puffs, around and around, from the bottom up. Then we decorated them with silver and gold candies, put mint leaves around the base and inserted little gold and silver candles to be lit before taking them to the tables. Now all I had to worry about were the dancers — could they carry the croquembouches to the tables without dropping them, or burning the place down?

The croquembouche matter resolved, I went upstairs to check on the room. Everything was perfect. The little gold chairs had arrived and were placed around the tables. The florist had delivered the red and gold poinsettias. The musicians were there and the harlequin dancers were dressing in one of the fifth-floor bedrooms.

It was 11 a.m. and all was well.

Wait!!! The illuminated balloons were not here yet!!! My heavens!!! Where were the illuminated balloons??? Where was Jack Frost???

I quickly ran to my office, called Jack Frost, but no one could give me an answer. I hung up in despair wondering what I was going to do. At about 11:30, the doorman called to tell me there was someone by the name of Jack Frost there wanting to come upstairs.

"Send him up! Send him up! Hurry! Send him up!"

Jack Frost got off the back elevator with all his equipment – gas tank, ladder, electric cords, Christmas lights — and balloons.

Soon, lighted balloons were strung around the pillars and up near the ceiling. The whole room looked like a Christmas display at Macy's — or, I should say, Marshall Fields.

Miss Hooper arrived promptly at noon. She stepped off the elevator, walked into the Silver Room and when she saw the illuminated balloons, she clapped her hands in glee.

At last I could relax. Now I knew the party would be a success.

Helen Rowntree

The Last Chapter

It's been a long while since Old Age crept up behind me,
nudging me down this darkening path.

Her quiet voice whispers soothingly:
"It's all right. Don't be afraid.
The last chapter is always the best.
Trees are never as eloquent
as when they turn red and gold.
And shortened days bring early stars.
When the sun departs behind brown hills,
it leaves a glorious trail of yellows, lilacs and pinks."

Proceeding with faltering steps,
I hear the crunching sounds
of dried memories, of faded loves
of past joys and retreating sadness.

It's all right. Don't be afraid.
The last chapter is yet to be written.
Words must be carefully chosen,
punctuation, precise and true.

At the end of this path is a gossamer door
set between the Here and the There.
When twilight dissolves into night,
when the familiar fades out of sight,
take my hand in Yours,
then wrap me in the nebula
of beginning again.

Joan Shepherd

Dick & Jane

I'm reporting on a book I read some time ago but have never forgotten.

It is an easy read, is well-illustrated and has action leaving you wanting more. The vocabulary is easy without any need of a dictionary to check on meanings.

The main characters are Dick and his friend Jane, whose names are the title of the book, *Dick and Jane*. Jane may be his sister in fact, but it doesn't matter if they are friends or related, because there is no hanky-panky in this story.

Dick has dark hair, as I remember, and is about 6 or 7 years old. Jane is no older. If these details sound vague, it is because it has been about 70 years since I read the book.

Action starts right away in the story, after we're asked to actually "see" Dick. And we can see Dick as there is a colored picture on the same page, which is Page 1.

Dick starts running, we don't know why, but the text says, "See Dick run" on Page 2, with a picture of Dick running. Is he running to meet Jane or just having a race with himself?

This is part of the intrigue of the book. We never find out why he is running, where he is going or if he ever got there.

On page 3, we meet Jane, "See Jane." Jane appears to be a sweet little girl wearing a dress, as when this book was written, no girls, young or mature, wore slacks or jeans or shorts. This indicates the book was written some time ago, something we wouldn't know with the few words we have read so far.

Jane meets Dick next and the drawing depicts the action. Following the theme of this book, guess what the words tell us?

"See Dick and Jane....run."

Was this a planned meeting? Are they running away? We have to be content just to know they can run–which, by the way, is more than this reporter can do at the present. It is a good thing there are illustrations as they add a lot to understanding the plot. Otherwise, it might be a bit boring.

Moving on, we meet Baby Sally, who appears to be about 18 months old. She has a chubby smiling face and blond natural curls. She is brought into the story sitting on a blanket and is concerned with playing with a ball. "Oh!" she says, as the ball in the picture rolls away. "Oh, oh".

Nobody in this tale ever shows any emotion other than pure joy in running, playing with a large rubber ball or with the final character, Spot the dog.

And you can guess what he looks like. Spot can run, too, which leads to him chasing the ball or simply running like Dick and Jane did at the beginning of the story. Maybe Spot is supposed to go find Dick and Jane.

We don't find out, but Baby Sally, who is alert and smiling, cheerfully says, "See Spot run," or for more emphasis, "Oh, oh, see Spot run."

I don't want to give the ending away, but since the story is based on a limited 8-10 words, there isn't much drama remaining. We may want to know if Spot did run away, since he is never on a leash, if Dick grows up to qualify for the Olympics, if Jane finds another friend to play with besides Dick and what that separation might create emotionally. Baby Sally? Her fate is wide open since her character is the least developed. As for Spot, dogs come and go and very few turn into a Lassie to make movies and a lot of money.

But the book *Dick and Jane* has been around for years. Thousands of adults and children have read it more than once, sometimes stumbling over the words but with a real sense of accomplishment when finished with the story because it could be the very first book they have read by themselves.

By the time a sequel of *Dick and Jane* as adults is written, it will undoubtedly have more words, perhaps even some dirty ones. And it will for surely have far more action.

Joan Shepherd

The Fly and I

Sick in bed, a fly lies beside me.
Then jumps to my other side.
I think this fly is trying to die.
So am I.

Joan Shepherd

Oh...Grandma

"Your Grandma has died," mother said as I came up the stairs from my bedroom. She had an expression on her face that I had never seen before.

Grandma was an old, bedridden woman needing to be fed pureed food and diapered for the past couple of years at our house.

I had never seen a dead person before. Now I would, in our back bedroom. I looked at her pale, frail body and touched her hand for a test. There was no reaction. Grandma was dead.

Grandma had no voice; she hadn't spoken in a long time. No more stories to tell about her eleven children or winning ribbons at the fair or how a mouse ran up her dress when in the tabernacle for a service. (She simply caught it in her skirt and held it until the service was over).

Instead of speaking, she tapped her gold wedding band on the metal side rail of her hospital bed. Tap...tap...tap...some sort of communication in her own Morse code. Tap...tap...tap, until the constant repetition so bothered my mother she removed the ring. Now Grandma wasn't tapping anymore. Nor was she wringing the sheet with her gnarled fragile fingers. Grandma was dead.

"Do I have to go to school today?" I asked. No, I didn't, but like Grandma, I couldn't say the words to tell my girlfriend why I was staying home. There was too much happening and I didn't want to miss anything. Grandma was dead.

The stretcher-like gurney squeezed through the narrow hall and came back with Grandma making a small lump under the sheet covering her. Grandma was dead.

I had seen enough. My emotions were fragile and I was embarrassed, with beginning tears. I went into the bathroom and cried.

Joan Shepherd

My Brain

My brain is convoluted
Sometimes, my thoughts are too
Twisted, curving, in and out
I don't know what to do.

But if my brain was smooth as glass
It would be so much worse
Thoughts would be even more contorted
Alzheimers being the curse.

An Expensive Present

Vic knew how to treat a woman. He might have read it in a book.

I learned fast that he had no trouble impressing women initially. I also learned only slightly later that the relationships didn't last.

I was one of those women.

After appropriate time exchanging emails and phone calls...yes, it was an internet arrangement...we met for lunch at a nice restaurant halfway between our separate cities.

I should have been more alert to the wide smiles of the staff greeting us as Vic, rather than the hostess, directed me to a private corner table. The table was already set with crystal glasses, a bottle of wine and a single rose across one menu. I knew which chair was mine.

Vic planned our dates thoroughly . . . knowing exact driving time, appropriate nearby restaurants, and even parking spots. He was never late either, which made him predictable and somewhat boring.

Still, I kept going with him because he did pick good places for dates (paying with one of several credit cards in his wallet secured with a rubber band). Frequently, he arrived with big beautiful bouquets of garden roses, which he later admitted were draped over his fence with his green-thumb neighbor. Or sometimes, with an unauthorized donation of roses from a local winery.

On some occasion, maybe a birthday or at Christmas, Vic gave me what looked like a credit card but turned out to be a gift card of $100 to Victoria's Secret. I'd never been to one of their stores, let alone know where one was!

He responded to my lack of enthusiasm with, "We'll find one," as if there was no hurry. So I tucked the card away and almost forgot about it.

Actually, I assumed Victoria's Secret was stocked with pornographic items which only depraved women would visit. I wasn't totally naive nor prim and proper, but the card remained untouched in my red wallet (which was intact with a snap).

During the next year or so, Vic occasionally would ask if I had been to Victoria's Secret. "No," I honestly answered, and it was no big deal.

But it came to pass one late afternoon that Vic pulled into a mall parking lot and pointed straight ahead saying, "See that store right ahead? That's Victoria's Secret. You are going in there to get something sexy. I'll wait outside."

The store was empty of customers but well stocked with a few young, slim, female clerks/models. They saw me but otherwise left me alone. I wandered about perusing lovely colored bras and underpants ranging from strings to bikinis to briefs. Also nighties, robes, and even more bras and panties. None were obviously pornographic nor even especially sexy.

I knew I couldn't leave empty-handed so I tried on and bought a two-piece outfit of black jersey-like fabric. The tap pants had pink dots and pink edging. The camisole had spaghetti straps loosely draping a solid top with enough to cover the midriff and was decorated by pink ribbon. Yes, not very sexy, but the outfit covered what needed to be.

I wore the outfit that night expecting Vic to turn away from the TV. He didn't. I sat beside him and he threw his muscular arm across my shoulders. During a commercial he asked with a smile on his face, "What did you buy today?"

"This is it!" I said.

His arm moved away for a better look. "I hoped you'd get black mesh hose with a garter belt and a black strapless bra!" was his obviously not-satisfied reply.

I was in my 70s at the time and had visible markings from surgeries that looked better covered with anything but black mesh.

It sounds strange but I would rather be naked than pretend I was Liza Minnelli in *Cabaret* singing some sexy song.

Good old Vic. He still loved me anyway, even for a while after I called an end to our adventure.

Maybe someday I will go back to Victoria's Secret and spend the card's remaining $20 or so on...anything but a garter belt.

Joan Shepherd

An Unexpected Stop

Resting my arms on the bathroom counter
contemplating life
a single ant came toward me
moving very quickly to some destination
which my arm obstructed.

It stopped, as if for a stop sign
and waited.

I lifted my drawbridge arm.

The ant shifted gears and sped forward
probably cussing his lost seconds.

Joan Shepherd

My Feet Took Me Walking

My feet took me walking tonight, independent of any directions.
It was a beautiful night to walk.
60 degrees, a half moon bright in a dark sky, a little breeze
which at first felt cool but later,
just a kiss on my face.

My feet took me walking tonight, they needed more exercise, I guess.
The hour was late which made it perfect for walking–
without cars or people.
Blinking blue and white lights flickered from windows in dark houses,
television for those whose feet wanted slippers,
not walking.

My feet took me walking tonight, directing themselves
because my mind was on other things.
It was so much on other things
that I walked right past my street without realizing it
until a couple of blocks later.
Good for my feet, knowing I wasn't ready to go home.

My feet took me walking past a convenience store
knowing I needed milk.
My feet remembered better than my brain.
Others made the bell ring as they entered the store
to buy lottery tickets, a pint of Jim Beam, cigarettes.
Milk is not a big selling item on a Friday night.

My feet went up a hill,
enough to make me a bit short of breath,
but that didn't slow their pace.

Joan Shepherd

Good feet. Good exercise.
And then they brought me down the hill
while I watched the half moon in the dark sky
without clouds on what had been a rainy day.

My feet were comfortable in my sneakers
but turned down my street anyway.
They knew it was time to go home.

When I entered the house, it was hot.
I had not worn a jacket and outdoors
the temperature was fine.
Inside, 68 degrees was way too warm.
But my feet were happy.

Both cats were asleep and didn't bother to greet me.
No messages from the phone or email.
This day has ended.

Thank you, feet.
Thank you, feet.

Joan Shepherd

Who Is That Woman?

Who is that woman sitting in the chair?
She kind of looks like my mother.
Her hair is full of soft white curls, so pretty.
Mother had beautiful hair.

Who is that woman drinking something?
It's Ensure! A nutritious drink, a little sweet.
My mother wouldn't like that.
She'd rather have a cold beer or a Coke.

Who is that woman sitting in the chair?
She seems to be talking to someone.
But no one else is there.
Mother talked on the phone a lot.
Especially to Aunt Emma and Aunt Cora.
Both of them worked.
Mother would often drive them home.

Who is that woman eating something?
Oh . . . Mother was such a good cook.
As a young girl, I would help her,
cutting up cabbage for coleslaw.
Mother loved coleslaw . . . and coffee.
She drank coffee all day long.

I moved closer to that woman sitting in the chair.
"Mother! It's me, Joan,
I've come from California to see you."
But she doesn't even look at me.
She is talking quietly to herself.

Joan Shepherd

"Mother." . . . My voice is a little shaky.
"Mom?" . . . I put my hand on her cheek,
to get her attention.
She casually brushes it away,
as if some fly has landed on her face.

Who is that woman sitting in the chair?
My aching heart makes the only possible conclusion.

She is not my mother.

Joan Shepherd

My First Job and Our Canary

When I was about 8 years old, I begged Mother for the job of giving the canary its bath. This was a tricky task with an element of danger for the bird if it escaped. Mother loved canaries, loved to hear them sing even if they interrupted *Helen Trent*, the soap opera she listened to. I got the job.

The bird seems a little apprehensive as I carry the cage to the kitchen table which is protected with old newspapers. One can use an official birdbath, about a 4-inch oval ceramic dish, or less sanitary but convenient, a cereal bowl from the cupboard. Filled with lukewarm water, it is placed some distance from the cage. Now comes the tricky part—slide out the bottom of the cage, making sure the bird is either on the swing or clinging desperately to the side. Holding the cage from the top or sides, quickly put the cage over the water dish and breathe a sigh of relief that the bird does not fly away in those seconds when escape is possible.

The bird may act as if it doesn't know what is happening but then suddenly, without any modesty, it will jump on the edge or into the bowl, flutter both wings in the water, splashing and ducking its head until satisfied it is clean and wet, maybe offering a short song of thanks when done. If left alone for a bit, the bathing may be repeated.

The supervisor of the bird's bath is not idle during this show. The debris at the bottom of the cage is removed, fresh newspaper applied and sprinkled with clean grit, which the bird may later scratch or even eat before the next housecleaning and bath.

Then, Dicky Bird, as my mother seemed to name each of her canaries, waits attentively as the process is reversed, an endeavor a little more threatening to an eight-year-old girl. The cleaned bottom tray has to be inserted into the cage, giving a bit more time for the canary to escape. The good thing is that Dicky Bird is usually happy after the bath and looking forward to a treat which will be provided–a dandelion, a piece of lettuce or a slice of apple stuck between the wires of the cage.

Canaries spend a lot of time exploring their homes, even on the floor where the grit and newspapers are. If they live long enough, they might learn to read. But these birds are meant to sing their little hearts out for others to hear and enjoy. And when they have eaten enough lettuce or dandelions and sung until their vocal cords become stiff with age, they go to the bottom of the cage, lie down and die.

That's what Dicky Bird did one day and that's where I found him– and experienced my first contact with death.

Joan Shepherd

Harboring a Secret

My sister Margaret told me a secret
and added, "Don't tell anyone."

The secret burns inside me now,
in my stomach and in my brain.
A neon sign flashes the tale,
while I do the dishes,
or shop for peanut butter.

I wish she hadn't told me,
and added, "Don't tell anyone."

They are words I don't want to hear,
because of course,
it's the first thing
I want to do.

I wish she hadn't told me,
and added, "Don't tell anyone."

I once knew a mother,
who told her troublesome first-grade son,
before he left for school:
"Don't throw rocks at people.
Don't take that rope to school,
to tie kids to the flagpole.
Don't ignore it when the teacher says,
'drink your juice nicely,
and don't spit it on the floor.'"

Of course, those are the very things
the kid did, like a good soldier,
following instructions.

I wish she hadn't told me,
and added, "Don't tell anyone."

OK, I've heard the secret,
and kept it within me,
for three and one-half days.
Haven't told a soul.
I've wanted to though,
because Lucy really needs to know.

I wish my sister had never told me her secret,
and added, "Don't tell anyone."

I haven't.

But, I probably will.

Joan Shepherd

First Rain

Dark gray clouds hung low all morning,
a dismal morning,
with a light globe trying to replace the sunlight.

My mind and feet are bored.
My eyes just keep watch on the weather.

Then the clouds lift a bit,
leaving dampness on the ground,
and a mist of rain in the air.

My feet move quickly,
barely giving my hands time to grab a jacket,
before we are outside.

I appreciate the fragrance of the first raindrops,
which had made tiny bowls in the dirt,
while giving thirsty grass a cool drink.

My feet are determined to move, without pause,
to explore the fresh scene.
Do my feet know where to go?
It seems like I am simply following them.
Yes, that is okay.

My cheeks dampen, with real rain.
It could have been from tears of joy
for the arrival, at last, of the rainy season.

I no longer resent the lack of sun.
I am no longer bored or restless.
I trust my feet to, without a plan,
take me for a wonderful walk,
in the rain.

Meta Strauss

Guardian of Love

At sunrise I took the secluded path to the beach and walked barefoot in the tranquilizing fringe of the surf. Breezes smelled like salt with overtones of seaweed and ozone. The sun warmed the air as I headed back home to my favorite deck chair and a stack of books I'd wanted to read. A pitcher of icy Mai Tai cocktails and a supply of snacks sat nearby.

I remember thinking that life could not be more perfect…. Now I have a new appreciation for moments of perfection and know they can vanish as fast as they occur, sometimes being replaced with regrets and profound sadness.

The day before the incident, I left my husband with our four-year - old twins in the city. I'd just completed architectural schematics for a major office building and was exhausted, ready to have a few days of peace and quiet.

Our beach house, my favorite place on earth, represents the best of my architectural creations. The gulf is visible from every room in the contemporary glass and cement structure but because of its position in a secluded cove hidden by sweeping dunes, plentiful shrubs and scattered juniper trees, neighbors or the few folks who wander the shore can't see it.

I hung my beach clothes on a peg under the stairs leading upward to a series of decks, then relished the feel of warm water pouring over my naked body in the outdoor shower. After slipping on a gauzy dress,

I enjoyed a Mai Tai with breakfast while watching seagulls weave in and out of the thermals.

On any given day, I see supply helicopters skirting the shoreline before heading to distant oil platforms. They usually travel alone so seeing three flying together was intriguing. Wanting to see more, I grabbed the binoculars beside my lounge chair and walked to the deck's edge.

They were military and flying in a triangular formation. Spellbound, I watched as they got closer and closer, entering the cove. They came so close to my house that I could see the crews without using my binoculars. They were young, good-looking guys wearing full gear like I'd seen in movies. I waved and smiled, leaning across the railing.

The name, *Guardian of Love*, was written in bright red across the side of the copter closest to me. The pilot turned and hovered mere yards away. He pointed, waved back, and smiled. His two team members joined in with smiles and waves as I threw a kiss to each and held up my glass in a toast.

It happened so fast! The other crafts turned. There was a bright white spark and a loud CRACK as the propellers of one clipped *Guardian of Love's* tail. The men's smiles vanished, replaced with wide eyes and opened mouths. *Guardian* spun in wild circles, the copter's tail flying away like a toy. I watched in disbelief as the entire craft morphed into a red ball.

My breath stopped as I watched the fiery mass disappear into the water. I think I screamed, but maybe I didn't make a sound. The other helicopters flew off at top speed. I ran back and forth on the deck and then down the stairs to the cove. I stood, staring at the water, feeling helpless.

I lost all sense of time. It probably was minutes but it seemed like hours when a larger helicopter appeared, motor roaring, circling, splashing water in all directions. Two men, garbed in scuba attire, dove into the cove where the sunken craft was located. Cables, giant claws, and netting surrounded the downed vehicle. After repeated dives, the scuba men were pulled back into the rescue copter. As if in slow motion, the *Guardian of Love* resurfaced. I could see the three men still strapped in, water pouring off their immobile bodies.

When the large craft flew away, a malfunction of some kind occurred and most of *Guardian* fell back into the water. The rescue team hovered, then left as fast as they had appeared. The cove waters stilled. The only noise was that of the surf on the beach and my own sobs.

The images of the men's faces kept playing in my mind like a horror film. With tears streaming down my face, I raced along the cove's path. I could see parts of the helicopter just under the water. I would have jumped in but I knew it was no use.

Once I regained my senses, I went to the house and using the landline, our only form of communication in the secluded area, I called 9-1-1. During the hour I waited for an ambulance and police to arrive, I called my husband and then downed a few Mai Tai to calm my nerves.

I showed the officials where the craft was but it could no longer be seen from our vantage point because of the incoming surf.

Writing information on a form, the lead officer shook his head. "Ma'am, we're in constant communication with the military bases in the area and there are no reports of a helicopter crash here or anywhere in the gulf today." When I argued he looked down at me and patted my shoulder. "Sometimes when a person is alone out here in the coves, they have delusions, maybe drink a bit too much." He pointed to my almost empty cocktail pitcher. "They see things that aren't there."

I was incensed. "That's ridiculous! I saw what I saw."

"I'm sure you think you saw something but we see nothing to confirm your report. Let us know if we can be of help another time." I watched them laugh as they drove away.

By the time Tom arrived, I was in tears again. I explained the police visit. He told of bypassing a roadblock but he saw nothing else that was unusual. We took our skiff out to the spot where the helicopter dropped the wreckage and Tom made his own underwater investigation. It was dusk but he could see the bodies of the men tangled in the wreckage.

We returned to the house to contact a friend at the television station for help. Before we could make the call, we heard a peculiar humming noise. We watched from our upper deck as an unusual military boat pulled into the cove. The watercraft resembled a submarine. It was oblong, shaped like an egg with a metallic dome on the top. Tom got his camera and videoed the operation while I took stills with my disconnected cell phone. The boat dragged the remains of the downed helicopter, along with the lost men, away from our cove, heading down the coast.

Minutes after the rescue boat left, two uniformed Navy officers, followed by a group of military types in full combat gear appeared at our door.

The lead officer identified himself as being with Homeland Security. He showed Tom an official-looking document, explained it was a search warrant, replaced it in his pocket, stepped inside, and beckoned to the others.

He addressed us like we were criminals. "This is about Homeland Security. We can't allow a preposterous story, like the one you told the police, to be circulated. Funds will be deposited in your bank account to cover the loss of confiscated items like cameras, phones and other recording equipment.

Tom tensed, hands clinched into fists at the sides of his body. I stood beside him shaking and crying as the group circulated through our home videotaping each room, opening doors, cabinets, drawers, tossing pillows, unmaking beds, even dismantling our barbeque.

By the time they completed the search, Tom was angrier than I had ever seen him. He screamed, "Get out of my home. Now! Look forward to hearing from the police, the FBI, the media, my attorney, the President and anyone else I can think of."

A military type grabbed him by his shoulders. "Shut the fuck up. Do not make any attempt to tell the media about the incident you think you witnessed. If you do, the story will be denied. We have the power to ruin you if you do."

The lead officer smiled, teeth showing like a toothpaste ad. "This is for your protection." He reached out to shake Tom's hand but my husband stomped to the door, opened it, and ushered the unwanted guests out.

During the next week we consulted our media friend as well as our family attorney explaining the events and our treatment. We didn't have a copy of the warrant or any photos, no proof anything occurred except for an anonymous deposit of eight thousand dollars that appeared in our checking account. They researched and found no evidence of the incident or that there was ever a helicopter with the unique name, *Guardian of Love*. The sheriff's office confirmed that a series of roadblocks were in place around our property that day, manned by the military, but it was explained as a training exercise.

After months of trying to find proof of the crash and the aftermath, we gave up. The bizarre incident ruined the serenity of our hideaway. Each time I sat on the deck of my beloved home or looked at the once peaceful cove, I remembered the explosion and the faces of the *Guardian of Love* men who died there as I toasted them. I had no way of contacting their families to tell them what I witnessed.

That spring when we put the house on the market, it sold in one day to an untraceable corporation and within days it was leveled. No explanation available.

The Last Kiss

I feel sunlight filtering through the oaks as a warm breeze crosses over my body. It's being guided directly to me, whispering, "Here is another day for you."

Bob has been sleeping in that chair for several nights now. Won't leave my side. If I could hold him in my arms I would, but I can't. I wonder if my thoughts get into his brain. There's still so much I'd like to say to him, like, "I feel like air. And, remember to eat leafy veggies and wear clean socks."

"Honey, are you awake?" He yawns, walks over to my bed, smiles, and strokes my head. "How would you like some ice chips?"

"Ummm. That's good," I say in my mind as it melts, dampening my dry mouth. I hope he gets the message.

Months ago Bob programmed my iPod, knowing my favorites would be welcomed later. Now, *Here Comes the Sun* plays quietly. Those Beatles wrote some great music. I remember how we downed rum and Coke and sang *Lucy in the Sky with Diamonds* at the tops of our out-of-tune voices, lined up with friends, arm in arm, swaying back and forth. Was that really forty years ago? What was the name of that bar? Oh, what difference does it make!

"Good morning," says Becky, my hospice nurse, walking in the door. Leaning over me while taking vital signs, she looks at Bob. "I think today might be her day. Is there anything I can do for you?"

He nods his head. "I want her to be comfortable. Do you understand? Very comfortable."

"Rachel, we'll keep you feeling good all the way. Just like we talked about," Becky's soft voice is soothing. She pulls my eyelids open, flashing a tiny light, testing my response. She smells like lavender and starch.

I AM FINE, I want to scream, but my voice doesn't work and my eyes won't open. But, my ears, they can hear a gardener clipping hedges three houses away. I noticed yesterday that I hear like an elephant. I think it was yesterday. Time means nothing now that there's none left. If I'd had this hearing all my life, just think what I would have overheard. At each of those lady lunches and office parties, I could have gathered news worthy of my own TV show.

"Hi, Dad. How is she doing this morning?" says my daughter, entering the room, arms filled with flowers, ribbons, and vases. Judy always has to have the surroundings look like a magazine picture. She strokes my brow, then takes my hand and rubs it. I want to hug her.

Nurse Becky motions to both of them and they go into the hallway. Of course I can hear every word they say and now, funniest thing, I can see them. It's kind of foggy, but there they are, standing together, Bob's arm around Judy's shoulder.

"Her vitals are slipping, her breathing is shallow, temp is low. Her circulation is beginning to slow. Now is the time to say your good-byes," Becky tells them.

I just hate this. Seeing them cry over losing me. It's more than I can bear. I escape through my window, soaring over the trees and the rose garden. What a glorious day. A young boy is pulling his wagon along the sidewalk, a little brown terrier jumping alongside. It's Charley when he was about six, with Trixie. I float over him and circle around our neighborhood, the old neighborhood where we lived before the kids grew up.

The music has changed to Frank singing,
"Come fly with me, let's fly, let's fly away
Once I get you up there where the air is rarified
We'll just glide, starry-eyed
Once I get you up there I'll be holding you so near
You may hear angels cheer 'cause we're together."

Beautiful. Yeah, Frank let's fly. I'm smiling. They're standing over me again. I wonder if they see it, that I'm smiling?

Judy grabs an emery board from her purse and begins filing my nails. I guess they're a mess. Bob peals the blankets off my feet and is massaging.

"Her feet are blue. What do you think?" he says to our daughter.

"You know she can hear us. Mom, can you hear us? Blink your eyes if you can hear us," says Judy.

I try as hard as I can but I have no control of my body anymore. I wish I could tell them I don't hurt. I don't feel a thing.

"Mom, we know you're ready, but please wait for Charles. He's on his way."

I have to stay for my Charley, but I look at the sky, the clouds, the sunrays, longing to touch them. They are so beautiful. I smell chocolate cake baking as I sail over our house. The yard needs mowing but is beautiful, so green. I'm holding a baby. It's Judy, and my mother and dad are laughing and pointing to her red hair. I'm at the high school stadium. There's Charley in his uniform, helmet off and he's being congratulated by his teammates. Judy is jumping up and down in her cheerleader outfit. Bob and I are laughing and hugging. We're young...and thin.

I soar like an eagle over a rainbow of purple, red, yellow, and pink tulip fields, weightless and nimble. Below me an immense emerald lake sparkles as if it's sprinkled with gold coins. The terrain changes to white peaked mountains. I ascend high into the atmosphere and immerse in white clouds. Like a circus performer I turn over and over, dart up and down in childlike delight. I watch a school of white dolphins play, jumping in unison as I float over warm gulf waters and back over the oaks. Bob is in his chair and Judy is arranging flowers while classical music plays.

I see his car pull into the driveway and watch Charley's nimble body sprint across the lawn, in the front door, and down the hall. All three stand beside my bed as Charley places his hands on mine and whispers into my ear. "I love you, Mom. I know I didn't say it enough, but you knew. I could always tell it in your eyes."

My eyes open and I smile. They see it. They see it this time! I focus on each of their faces. They smile back and then laugh, better than any music. They become mist, an illusion, an impression.

I slip out the window like a bubble, sailing far above the oaks, orbiting into the clear blue sky, singing and giggling as I pass the towering Cascades, the endless Pacific, the vast African plains.

My essence, the "me only I know," is embraced by the stratosphere. Textures, fragrances, colors and light connect like a boundless work of art, fusing with the echo of continuous tones, and limitless melodies, a million voices overflowing, resonating, powerful. We all combine into a massive vibration that is all, is nothing, united, eternal.

"She's gone." Judy sobs as Bob cradles her.

Charley puts his arms around both. "Did you feel it? The warm breeze? Just as she took her last breath?"

"Yes." Bob closes his eyes as his thoughts caress the air. "That was her last kiss."

The Note

Like the first Saturday of every month, Roger Whitney left the neighborhood barbershop to meet his men's group. He sported the same haircut he had for the past forty years. "If it works, then why change?" he said to the mirror as he spread Brylcreem through his graying hair.

As Roger sat drinking coffee at the Uptown Bakery, waiting for his friends, the same buddies he'd had most of his life, he wondered whom his wife had invited for dinner. Her list of friends was long, and changed as often as the seasons. The truth was that Marjorie liked variety. She spent most of her time and their money redoing and then redoing again. He didn't think she wore the same clothes twice, or at least he couldn't tell if she did, and her hair had been so many colors he wasn't sure what was natural.

One day a couple of years ago he came home from a business trip and drove right past their house. A new porch, paint job and landscape made it look so different he didn't recognize his own home.

After coffee, a Danish, and discussions with the group, Roger went to the hardware store, another Saturday ritual. This time he brought his general-purpose hammer with him to get the handle replaced. It would be ready in an hour. He glanced in store windows as he walked along the street and tried to understand why people, especially Marjorie, had to transform the world on a regular basis.

He almost passed up the car forgetting his truck was in the shop and that he was driving Marjorie's BMW, something he didn't like to do. He was comfortable with his Ford pickup, not hot-rodding around in a convertible, a red one, at that.

He fumbled for the remote control starter device, aggravated that the new car didn't even use keys. It was then he noticed a paper stuck under the windshield wipers. "Damn advertisement," he said, carefully removing it. He frowned thinking about the people who place flyers under blades and how they should know this causes pressure on the rubber, enough so that they no longer work properly and had to be replaced. It was a conspiracy. The flyer was probably put there by the auto supply store.

However, when he looked closer, he realized the flyer was not a flyer. It was a neatly folded handwritten note. He slid back into the driver's seat, put on his reading glasses and opened it. *"Dearest one, I looked for you when I saw your car, but couldn't find you. I was hoping to steal a kiss. I have a last-minute appointment and can't meet you at our regular place. I'll be crazy until I see you! All my love, XX"*

Roger read the note again. Then again. And again. "Who would leave me a note like this?" He took off his glasses and rubbed his eyes. The handwriting was neat. No misspelled words. There was no doubt it was from a lover and he didn't have one, other than Marjorie.

He frowned as another thought entered his mind. "This is Marjorie's car. What if the note wasn't meant for **me**?" He hit the steering wheel with his fists.

He got out of the car searching for a suspicious-looking man. "Yes," he said to himself. "This note was meant for Marjorie and is from **her** lover!" He almost cried. His hands shook so much he dropped the starter gadget and had to crawl under the car to find it.

"How could she? But then again, why wouldn't she?" Roger knew he was set in his ways, but it had never occurred to him his wife would toss him out of her life like she did everything else.

He thought about last winter when Marjorie's best friend was Lydia Marshall, a woman who taught some kind of jewelry class. She was at their home every morning. When he left for work the two women would be talking, laughing and drinking coffee while they set boxes full of beads on the dining table. One day the project was gone. Marjorie explained she was bored with jewelry making. Two days later a woman named Betty or Beatrice or something was there with a yoga mat. Marjorie was dressed in stretchy workout gear, was playing an Eastern-sounding CD, ready to meditate. About a month ago the yoga teacher was out and Marjorie was off on a new bicycle with Judith somebody or other.

"What if I'm like these friends? Obsolete. Out-of-date. Not the flavor of the month," he continued talking to himself. He was certain. She had found somebody else. He had warnings from her all along. From the beginning of their marriage she told him he was stodgy, too dependable, inflexible. He should have seen it coming.

He backed the car out of the space looking around for XX, whoever he was. He turned into traffic and drove away. Fast. Then faster. And faster. He went through town and continued past the city limits. He lost track of time and space. His brain was a land mine exploding with memories.

He thought of his first day at work many years ago when he fell in love at first sight. Marjorie had handed him a clipboard. "Welcome to Brazos Engineering," she said with a smile as beautiful as a toothpaste ad. "Please fill out these forms." He watched as she worked, sorting files, tapping her pen on the desk, answering the phone, crossing and uncrossing her legs, all the while turning in her swivel chair. When her blouse fell open exposing significant cleavage, he had a difficult time concentrating on the paperwork. He knew someone like him, a certified nerd that carried a slide rule in his pocket, didn't stand a chance with a dish like the boss's sexy assistant.

Yesterday should have alerted him that their marriage was in deep trouble. Marjorie used a screwdriver and left it on the kitchen drain board instead of returning it to the outlined slot on the tool board in his workshop. He made a big deal of it.

She shouted at him. "You are a fuddy-duddy, always having to keep things in exactly the same place."

He had been firm. "You are messy, leave stuff all over instead of doing the simple and practical task of keeping things in order."

"Damn it to hell!" He was jolted back to reality when the car crashed into a barrier that stretched across a dirt road. A stunned Roger turned off the engine, slipped out the door, zigzagging to the front of the car to assess the damage. He leaned against the bashed bumper, his head spinning. He was sure the front end would have to be replaced. Looking around at the surrounding forest, he realized he had no idea where he was and no inkling how long he'd been there. He sunk to the ground, devoured by more memories.

He heard about Marjorie's interest in ballroom dancing from another Brazos Engineering employee. His dancing was mediocre at best, so he went to the local Arthur Murray Studio and took a few lessons. As he waited by her desk for the boss, he mentioned how he liked to dance. The next evening he had his first date with Marjorie.

Four months after their first date Marjorie decided the two of them should take up tennis. She signed them up for lessons and bought rackets for their new endeavor. When he inquired about dancing she said she wanted to concentrate on tennis instead. He wanted to concentrate on Marjorie and did just that for the next twenty-four years.

He shook his head, struggled up and untangled the car from the barrier. Thank goodness the damaged auto ran. He followed the road until it hit the main highway. When he looked at the dashboard clock he realized it had been hours since he found the note. The hammer would be ready. He headed back to town.

When they'd been dating for a year she decided a trip to Las Vegas would be fun. The trip ended with them in a wedding chapel wearing matching gold bands.

He loved Marjorie, never looked at another woman. He couldn't imagine kissing anyone else. How could **she**? His mouth was dry. His heart beat so fast he thought he would have a heart attack. "When I find out who 'XX' is, I'll...."

He found a parking space, the same one he'd had that morning. "I'll get the damned hammer and then go home and confront Marjorie." Instead, he went to the barbershop.

"What are you doing back, Roger? Forget something?"

"Nope, George, can you do anything different with my hair?"

"Huh? You've had the same cut all your life, I think."

"Yeah, I want something new, different."

Within thirty minutes Roger was transformed. His style was a duplicate of Brad Pitt's on the cover of *People* magazine and his color was bleached from brown to blond.

He went in the shoe store and a few minutes later walked out wearing orange Nike Airs. Seeing his image reflected in the store's window, the new Roger swaggered back to the car ready to challenge Marjorie.

"Hey! Mister!" A young woman ran after him. Her uniform had *Marilyn's Beauty Emporium* embossed above the pocket. "Wait! Please wait."

Roger stopped. "Do you mean me?" Maybe the hair was attracting young women. He couldn't know for sure. He stopped at his car and realized it wasn't his car but an identical car *without* the bashed grill. A handsome man got out and joined the woman. As Roger digested the situation, the woman continued to talk.

"I'm SO glad you came back to town. You were here this morning, right?"

"Yes."

"I wasn't sure because of the smashed front end of your car."

"Yeah," he grimaced.

"See, this morning I saw your car and I thought it was my boyfriend's. You didn't by chance find a note stuck under your wipers?"

Roger nodded his head. "Yeah. I did."

"See, Charlie, I did leave you a message." The woman spoke to her boyfriend.

Roger grabbed hold of the car door to steady himself and took a deep breath. He reached into his pocket and handed the folded paper to the couple.

As they walked away, Roger stared wide-eyed, thinking about the note. He looked down at the bright orange shoes and ran his hands through his short, spiky blonde hair. He laughed out loud, for the first time in a very long time.

Roger made one more trip down the sidewalk and bought a dozen long-stemmed red roses. Then he got into the wrecked BMW and drove home to Marjorie.

Fond Farewell

The aging population in our small town makes it a certainty that we have a regular supply of deaths. Because we're short on social activities, funerals are entertainment–opportunities to get together, share news, eat some snacks, and dress in something other than jeans.

Dixie Marie Higgins's service drew a bigger than usual crowd. She was *that woman*: the one everyone liked to gossip about, *the woman* women forbid their husbands to be around. But, I knew her good side and all the sadness she'd endured. We'd been friends since grade school.

"Dixie Marie has more flowers than I thought she would, given her lifestyle." Bonnie McKenzie was one to always voice an opinion.

"Bonnie, you know flowers are not given so much to honor the deceased as they are to make the giver feel good. Often they make up for feelings of guilt," I said.

She said, "How did you come by that information?"

"It's common knowledge. Pure psychology."

"Damn it, Fran," she said. "You always have to make like you know more than me, no matter what."

I couldn't argue that, so I said. "Look at this beautiful giant spray of carnations. They're from someone who signed the card *Love Forever, S.M.* No real name."

"Hmmm," she said. "*Love Forever, S.M.* That could be anyone."

I said, "Sam or Stanley or Steve...no one comes to mind right off that I ever heard Dixie talk about."

"Oh my. Look at these lovely yellow roses. The card is from...guess who? S.M. And here's another from S.M."

"There must be a half dozen bouquets from him. He must've thought she was special."

"No shit," said Bonnie.

"This is a real mystery. I should know the person who loved Dixie enough to send all these flowers. She was my good friend."

"That's true. I thought she told you everything. So, are you going to view Dixie Marie with me?"

"I don't do dead bodies of any kind. You know that, Bonnie."

"Well, I want to see what her sister laid her out in and how in the hell they fixed the hole."

"You go look, then tell me. I'm betting she's wearing her baby blue suit. It's the only decent thing I ever saw her in. You know Dixie Marie. Most of her wardrobe wouldn't do for burying purposes."

"I'm thinking that jealous bitch sister of hers probably kept the blue suit for herself and put Dixie Marie in something she knew she would hate."

"Un-huh," I said, nodding. "I'll meet you at the coffee area by the cookie table. Don't puke when you see Dixie Marie." I watched Bonnie walk away, smiling at first one friend and then another. While Bonnie did her body-viewing, I listened to the gossip. Everyone knew that Dixie Marie went out with a bang. Literally. Held a pistol behind her right ear in front of a dozen people at the Back Street Bar. Then she yelled, "Fuck them!" and pulled the trigger.

"I've had three cups of coffee and two trips to the Ladies." I said, "What took you so long, Bonnie?"

"Girlfriend, it was just too sad. Bless her heart; Dixie Marie didn't even look like herself."

"What did you expect? She was screaming when she passed. That can't make for a nice dead body."

"And, just like I thought, that bitch kept the blue suit," Bonnie said. "She had Dixie Marie dressed in some kind of pink satin robe with pink earrings, pale pink lipstick painted on. Didn't even look like her real lips. And, her hair was styled all curly, with bangs spread across her forehead."

"Well, I understand the bangs. How else do you think they could show her? Having a bullet go though your head would cause major damage."

"Fran, you couldn't even tell about the hole in her head. I heard they filled it up with plaster and then painted it to look just like her skin."

"I'll bet you could see the repair if you looked close," I said.

"They say where the bullet goes out is where the big mess is. Like JFK. Blew off the whole back of his head. There were parts of his brain all over the limo, on the Secret Service men, not just on Jackie's pink suit. Dixie Marie had a similar situation."

"I think the hole was smaller coming from a revolver," I said.

"Maybe. Have you tried the lemon bars?"

"They're so good with fresh hot coffee." I smiled at Dottie Watkins who was serving refreshments.

"Only she shot herself close-up. The bartender said she sprayed the bar, fellow customers, the plate-glass window and a rack of whiskey bottles."

"I told you, I want to remember Dixie Marie like she was in life. Beautiful and wearing party clothes. Your memory will be scarred."

"The only thing bad in that casket was the pink outfit. Dixie Marie never would have worn pink."

"No. Not her style at all," I said.

We followed the crowd into the sanctuary. The preacher always delivers a set funeral sermon and only changes it up enough at each service to make it seem he deserves the four hundred dollars he charges.

Bonnie whispered, "Reverend Duvall is making Dixie Marie out to be a saint."

I whispered back, "The truth is she *was* a saint back in high school. I'm glad folks are reminded she was class beauty and an honor student."

"That was before her jealous bitch sister fucked her over. Lou Anne had already fucked the entire football team, so why not her sister?"

"Now, watch your language. We're in church," I said.

"I do wonder who told the Reverend these stories about Dixie Marie's family background."

Bonnie whispered back that she was sure it was Lou Anne. "She always has to pretend her family is better than anyone else's, like they're the town's high society."

I agreed. "Those girls were poor farm girls. Lou Anne was notorious from the beginning and everyone knows the bitch was responsible for causing Dixie Marie's downfall."

"Well, in the end, Dixie Marie made more married men happy than anyone else in town."

After the service we went back to the church community room for more refreshments. Bonnie said, "Do you see that snake, Ralph Leigh, here with his wife?"

"You think the Mrs. knows about him and Dixie Marie screwing around?"

"Hard to say."

"Everyone else in town knows, but maybe she doesn't want to," I said.

"Or maybe she's here to be sure Dixie is dead and gone from her life. Then old Ralph will return to screwing her."

"These little chocolate cupcakes are really good. Try one," I said.

"They are de-lish. The Reverend's wife made them. I've seen at least four of Dixie's former companions here with their wives. Wonder which one has the initials S.M.?"

"The tiny tuna sandwiches are a nice touch," I said.

"I think Dixie did it with everyone because she was lonely, no husband of her own, and haunted by memories of how she lost Robert," Bonnie said.

"There's Lou Anne, acting like she's all sad."

"Royal bitch. Two-faced. Viper. Wiping made-up tears from her eyes with a damn lace handkerchief."

"I've hated her forever," I said. "Robert and Dixie Marie were the perfect couple. Everyone said so."

"It's pure town history," Bonnie said. "Lou Anne took Robert home after class and screwed him in Dixie Marie's twin bed. Not hers, but her own sister's! She timed it so when Dixie Marie walked in from school she'd find them huffing and puffing. The bitch on top, naked."

I said, "You are right. All her life since, Dixie Marie had to look at the two of them together at family reunions, knowing she was the one who should have the big house. She should have been Sadie, Sadie, married lady."

"Robert is a damned idiot, always has been."

"Hope he feels guilty about this. You want another brownie?" I grabbed another off the table.

"No, I've had my fill." Bonnie sipped on another cup of coffee. "Don't count on either one of them feeling bad about hurting Dixie Marie. Look at him laughing and stuffing one of the lemon bars in his big mouth."

At that moment it hit me who S.M. was. I wished Dixie Marie had aimed the pistol at both of them instead of herself.

Bonnie and I stood in the receiving line a long time. It gave us a chance to plan the perfect condolence message to the bereaved couple.

First Bonnie hugged the super bitch and then Robert the cheater. I did the same. We both did our best real sad looks and said, "We're so sorry for your loss."

Bonnie added, "Lou Anne, Dixie Marie looked so beautiful all fluffed out in that angel pink gown. I guess you knew that pink was her favorite color."

Then, I smiled especially big and said, "Robert, it was very sweet of you to send so many flowers in honor of Dixie Marie." I loved seeing the shocked look and the tears running down his face.

Watching to be sure that Lou Anne could see her husband, Bonnie said, "And, for you to use your S.M. code name from way back in high school was really special."

I patted his hand. "Dixie Marie told me you were always her number one 'Super Man,' better than all the rest put together." I smiled again. "I'm sure Dixie Marie has found peace at last but I have to wonder if you two ever will."

Then Bonnie and I walked away with Lou Anne's screeches echoing in our ears.

Dixie Marie's funeral was the best ever and she deserved it.

Janet Wentworth

Janet Wentworth

Janet Wentworth

Just a Minute!

minutes like pennies
add up
a day, a week, a month
a life time fortune

just a minute
to send that email
life time to live with it

just a minute
to say I do
a life time to live
with him or her

just a minute
to conceive a child
a lifetime to live
with him or her

just a minute
to write this
dumb poem!

Janet Wentworth

It's in the Book

according to the Bible
you should not put the new wine into
old skins

when you are thin
and young
it is okay to imbibe
new wine

but beware

when you are plumper than thin
older than young
more wrinkled than smooth

some new wine will
cause you to whine
and cry about your life of strife

the problem is
new wine is cheaper
than old

Janet Wentworth

Star Gazing

when I look
upon a star
I often wonder
who I are

My Bed

There was a beetle in my bed
Why couldn't it have been a man instead
I see a bug and lose my head
I could feel a man
And lose my heart

Metaphors

what are they for
to brighten thoughts
why add more

confuse issues
layer emotions
spice the stew
sprinkle like salt
a very few

keep it clear
just say it
damn it

Janet Wentworth

Turtles

how to live longer
what the scientists
attempting to define

turtles live the longest
they have a shell
turtles can hide
when life is hell

turtles move slow
because they know
fast won't last

Apples

apples appear every year
the universe
always on time
round and good
the apple is the universe

1906

Nellie Goodloe, my grandmother, thought she would never live to see the day when one of her paintings would place third in the 1916 San Francisco Exposition.

One night in April, years before the exposition, in the year 1906, she was awakened by the sound of her daughter screaming and her husband pounding up the stairs to her daughter's bedroom. Her bedroom floor was heaving and there was a piercing sound of cracking as the building swayed back and forth.

Shaking with fear, Nellie managed to crawl through the enveloping darkness to the front hall where she found her husband, Paul, and her teenage daughter, Clarascott.

As they heard a crashing sound of bricks tumbling down the roof and saw them flying past the window to the street, Paul shouted, "We have to get out of here now, this is one hell of an earthquake."

The trembling threesome slid down the shaking stairs leading to the front door on their behinds. Fortunately the door was not jammed so they could continue their sliding process down the outside stairs to the sidewalk.

Paul said, "We need open space, let's head down the street to the Chinese vegetable garden."

Clad only in their nightclothes, and clutching each other, Paul, Nellie and Clarascott walked cautiously the 200 yards towards the vegetable garden. They were able to stand upright as the ground had stopped heaving and shaking.

There was an eerie silence in the neighborhood, punctuated by the shrill shriek of distant sirens. The acrid smell of smoke wafted towards them as they pushed open the garage-like door behind which lay the vegetable garden.

Nellie: "Paul, is the city burning?"

"Nellie, I know as much as you do. It certainly sounds and smells like it. We are better off here until we find out. God save us and our property."

Nellie, Paul and Clarascott huddled together, shivering in the midst of rows of zucchini, cauliflower and tomato plants in the tennis court-size garden (which it eventually became) for what seemed hours.

Finally, hearing sounds of activity on the street, the three ventured outside. There were people crowding a truck delivering tents for those made homeless by the earthquake.

Paul grabbed a tent although their large shingled building look intact except for the chimney bricks scattered around.

It was decided that Paul and Nellie would venture into their apartment separately for their clothes and some supplies, as they didn't want to both die if it collapsed and leave Clarascott an orphan.

Paul noticed the front outside stairs were slightly askew, but the front door opened and the inside stairs to the front hall seemed intact. There were large cracks around the fireplace in the living room to the left of the hall.

Paul recalled that when he had the four-unit, two-story building constructed in 1902, the entire building was attached to the brick fireplaces in each unit. Although the chimneys had collapsed, the brick fireplaces seemed intact, but he decided they couldn't risk it. The smell of burning buildings seemed to be getting stronger.

Paul collected supplies and clothes for himself and Clarascott for a camp-out in the vegetable garden.

When Nellie gingerly entered their apartment, hastily collecting clothes and some family keepsakes, she was dismayed to see her artwork and china scattered across the floor.

As the family moved into the vegetable garden, ashes and a cloud of smoke puffed around them, wafting from the house fires burning on the other side of Van Ness Avenue.

Paul immediately set to work setting up camp while Nellie brewed some coffee over an open fire. The aroma of morning coffee brought some sense of normalcy to the bizarre setting.

Paul, ever positive, said, "At least we will have vegetarian diet and I brought enough butter to last a week. Hopefully the fire won't cross Van Ness and we will soon be able to repair Filbert Street."

The four-unit Filbert Street building, a short distance from the Palace of Fine Arts, location of the 1916 Exposition, stands intact to this day. Nellie's oil painting of their Cupertino ranch won third prize.

Air in My Tires

stop sign
in my computer
writing signs
in all directions

brain with a flat tire
which signs to follow
childhood, school
marriages, career

tragedy & joy
writing professor
my passenger

Janet you know
what directions
to take

You have the gas

Janet Wentworth

My Building of Memories in Cow Hollow

first memory
four years old and visiting
grandparents Paul and Nellie Goodloe
2391 Filbert Street in San Francisco
Paul built the apartment building in 1902
holding my hand tightly
towering above me
we walked down Filbert Street
for treats at the corner ice cream store

in the middle of the block
I felt a kick on my right leg
someone is kicking me
I cried out in indignation
Paul looking down at me with a smile
peering around up and down
now who could that be

as we entered the ice cream store
I glimpsed Paul raising and bending
his right leg
oh! Grandpa you kicked me
laughing, he said, "you caught me"

Paul was a ham, playing little jokes
leftovers from childhood on an
Alabama cotton plantation
raised with six siblings
he was fun

Erase & Repair

memories
three husbands erased
my first husband's obit
second family

"dreamer, thinker
and consummate reader"

and there he is

Squaw Valley chairlift in the forties
consummate reader
power skiing on the way up
a quick study for the way down

crashed six feet four
in the middle of downhill
skiing class
ski instructor & author of "Power Skiing"

a broken leg for repair

Landmark Mailing

yesterday
twenty one years after husband
Chapman II's death

I mailed nephew Chapman III
his heirloom watch

Edward Kirk Chapman I
his death at 87
reported in the Portland, Maine
paper 1862

Known as king of Christmas
Tree dealers and Lieutenant
of Santa Claus

Checker Champion of the
State of Maine & Civil War Veteran

scribbled note
of my husband reads

given to Edward Kirk Chapman
by President O.C. Posten
of Maine Railway

I don't know why
colorful Chapman memory
tucked away all these years

felt good to let you go
E.K. Chapman
where you belong

Stealing Time

how to live longer and be stronger
what the scientists are attempting to define

what an irony
watching a French lady
celebrate her 126th birthday on T.V.
while holding a 3-month-old baby
in my arms

The skin is the first to go,
according to the channel 9 documentary on aging.

What will Whitney Wisnom look like in a hundred years?
What will her world be like in a hundred years?

Whitney Wisnom might live to be a hundred.

A few generations ago her ancestors only made it to 46.

Janet Wentworth

The Wind in My Hair

"where is your helmet?" "I don't care
I want the wind in my face
and through my hair"

he sat in front of that Reno bank
his motorcycle engine roaring
"I don't need a helmet/to hell with it
being the law"

"I want the wind in my face
and through my hair"

discharged from his navy ship
he had driven his cycle from San Diego

we saw him soaring
around the sharp curves
of the mountain
as we followed in
our little Mustang

the wind whipped through his hair
reddening his happy face

why a cycle?
we had asked desperately

"I want the wind in my face
and through my hair"

the wind was blowing
over his face and hair
he lay still
on that fatal hill

Note: David, my son, age nineteen, had just returned from Vietnam on the USS Ticonderoga.

Janet Wentworth

Three Ways of Looking at a Pigeon
(while living at Lake Tahoe)

on our deck one morning
sat a pigeon
with an air of permanence

I was of a different mind
like a mother who has lost a son

the pigeon still sat there
in the setting sun

a mother and a son
a man and a woman
a pigeon and a spirit
are one

I did not know what to see
a pigeon
or the spirit of my son

snow started to fall softly
it was the end of fall
the pigeon still sat there

then we could see
thru the dim light
it was a carrier pigeon
where did it come from
where was it going
did it bring a message
from another dimension

the lake was churning
the clouds were darkening
the wind was howling
the pigeon still sat there

the next day dawned
a dark and stormy morning
our messenger pigeon
was gone

a spirit messenger
a lost pigeon

or my missing son

Clouds

when I fly above the clouds
my heart gives out
I gave you to the universe
when we flew above the clouds
we dropped your ashes from the sky
I am totally without
your warm embrace and loving eyes
I can only hope your spirit
is somewhere high
you will always be in my ear
you made that promise before you died
one thing is sure/you never lied
please send your spirit so I can hear
rid me of my fear

Janet Wentworth

Life Instructions

life doesn't come with instructions
we are all producers
of our own productions

scene one
when we are born

final scene
when we are old
and begin to mold

but not for long
we reappear
in different form

who knows
what that will be

someone/something
we cannot see
when we are here

Janet Wentworth

Rush

the internet gold rush
bigger/better
God, take a letter
what will happen
to us

we're falling
off the planet
damn it!

Zigzagging

it's running
not thinking
it's zigzagging!
you put something there
then you don't know where
it's zigzagging!
seize the emotional moment
write a note
your friend or relative
becomes remote
it's zigzagging!
email is worst
write in a hurry
just press send
your message is off
so is your friend

it's zigzagging!
it's a small disease
not at ease
with yourself
"cannot see the forest for the trees?"
it's zigzagging!
point A to point B
is not a straight line
and harder to define
it's zigzagging!

Dust Our Destiny

the war was far away
when I was young
now graphic images speed
around our planet

blood drips from my computer
stories of personal disaster
death & destruction of civilians
little children in shock

modern technology
drives my cell/computer
steers missiles
over there
hope in a news report
cell phone videos of war
let internet viewers hear
the rockets, feel the terror

hope that our technology
can guide us to compassion
love instead of fight
before our planet explodes
and dust our destiny

Swimming with Sharks

top of the news
investors lose

I lost a lifestyle
for a lifetime

a scam real estate exchange
left me with little change

so those days are gone
a picture of me in Mexico
now

after corporate crunch
it's only lunch

business
an organized way to steal
by more than
one heel

sorry about that
say the corporate highs
we didn't mean
to lie

Janet Wentworth

the CEOs
live like kings
or so I am told

as lawsuits unfold
their souls might
turn to mold

is it too much to ask
that these principals
be taken to task

if I am bitter
it is the moral litter
some executive crooks
have strewn about
before they were
finally found out

so it goes
for corporate greed
sleazy souls
who have the need
for bigger mansions
a lot of green

Janet Wentworth

Mourning Myself

taking my death seriously
seems improbable
nineties already
how did that happen

where did those years go?
taking my death seriously
I'm told is important
while still alive
sign new documents
smooth the way for my daughters
while I can
I will miss myself!

About the Authors

Russ Bedord has degrees in Mechanical Engineering and English and is unreasonably proud of being a Yooper. He writes in different formats of prose and poetry, some published. He was winner of the 'Poet as Community Leader' award.

Noris Binet is a visual artist, poet, author and spiritual teacher and is a native of the Dominican Republic. She offers her dharma poetry to assist meditation and self-inquiry and has contributed to *The Sonoma Sun*, *Sonoma Index-Tribune*, and the bi-lingual *La Voz* newspapers.

Joan R. Brady has been writing since the 1970s and is a poet and produced/published playwright. Her work has appeared in the United States, Scotland and Paris. She has published two books, *The Space Between* (2010) and *Persona* (2014).

John Field left Iowa after graduating from college and went west to teach high school in California. After retiring, his passions lie in writing poems, listening to jazz, reading novels and enjoying his wife Mary's gardening. He constantly enchants the writers with his "1,000 picture metaphors."

Lucille Hamilton grew up on the New Jersey cliffs opposite NYC. After college she worked in London, Rome and Vienna and, on returning to the USA, became an RN. Upon retiring she came to Sonoma, CA, and finally found time for writing with the Sonoma Writers Alliance.

Michael James describes his biography as Chaucer might have done. "Mined in England, there thrown on the wheel for impress of first hands, turned and shaped in Berkeley, and fired and painted by students of Tamalpais (school) district," which he left in 1993. He writes essays, stories, and poetry.

Beverly Koepplin was raised in Montana and transplanted to San Francisco, California, in 1966, where she found herself (literally and figuratively) a flower child whose spirit still reigns supreme. She writes for pleasure. Her poetry has been published locally and she is preparing to publish her first novel.

Dave Lewis is a Wisconsin farm boy who morphed into a Mechanical Engineer. After 35 years in the design of rocket and jet engines, he retired and finally found California and an opportunity to write fiction instead of facts.

Robyn Makaruk, born in New Zealand, flew the coop to the U.S. in 1963 and gravitated to California in 1971. Her lifelong love of the written word in its many forms gives her the opportunity to express her own take on quirky and reflective prose and poetry.

Michael Miley. In keeping with his fascination with the paranormal (shamanism, near-death experiences, UFOs, psychic research, the phenomenology of psychedelics and altered states), Michael has a love for experimental fiction and poetry. He feels that his efforts capture less than 10% of the strangeness of the world.

Ellie Portner was born and raised in Montreal, Quebec, Canada, and currently shows her artwork at the Sonoma Arts Guild in Sonoma, CA. Her interests include writing poetry, drawing, painting, travel, singing and playing the ukulele.

Helen Rowntree was born in San Francisco. She lived in El Salvador and Chicago, then returned to California in 1986. Her life has been so varied, she has lived at least eight lives. An original member of the Sonoma Writers Alliance, she began writing for pleasure in 1993 and hopes to complete her memoir in this lifetime.

Joan Shepherd. When in high school, a story she wrote for her English class was selected to be included in a booklet. After retiring from several careers, she spent more time writing and creating art. She is writing to have her English teacher give her an "A" again and select a piece for another booklet 60 years later.

Meta Strauss moved to Sonoma from her lifelong home in Houston, Texas, in 2005 and began writing. Her work appears in local papers and she reads at area events. She was published in the anthology *Cry of the Nightbird*, and her family tales appear in *Stories for Emma*. Meta's first novel, *Saving El Chico*, was published in early 2016.

Janet Wentworth. A fourth-generation San Franciscan, she had a long career in public relations in the Bay Area and Tahoe. She brings a writing style with the punch of the newsroom and peppered with humor. Her writings can be found in the recently published book *Under the Redwoods*.

Made in the USA
Charleston, SC
20 February 2017